RD013880

D1140454

Dumfries and Galloway Libraries, Information

This item is to be returned on or before the last date
shown below.

DUMFRIES AND
GALLOWAY LIBRARIES
WITHDRAWN

306.8742

Dumfries and Galloway
LIBRARIES
Information and Archives

Awarded for excellence in public service
Dumfries and Galloway
Libraries, Information and Archives

Central Support Unit: Catherine Street Dumfries DG1 1JB
tel: 01387 253820   fax: 01387 260294   e-mail: libs&i@dumgal.gov.uk

24 HOUR LOAN RENEWAL BY PHONE AT LO-CALL RATE · 0845 2748080
OR ON OUR WEBSITE · WWW.DUMGAL.GOV.UK/LIA

how to be a great

divorced
dad

simon baker
with alley einstein

AS | Dumfries and Galloway LIBRARIES

| | 0 | 1 | 3 | 8 | 8 | 0 | 306.874^2 |

foulsham
LONDON • NEW YORK • TORONTO • SYDNEY

foulsham

The Publishing House, Bennetts Close, Cippenham, Slough,
Berkshire, SL1 5AP, England

Foulsham books can be found in all good bookshops and direct from
www.foulsham.com

ISBN: 978-0-572-03368-2

Copyright © 2007 Simon Baker and Alley Einstein

Cover photograph © Superstock

A CIP record for this book is available from the British Library

The moral right of the author has been asserted

All rights reserved

The Copyright Act prohibits (subject to certain very
limited exceptions) the making of copies of any
copyright work or of a substantial part of such a work,
including the making of copies by photocopying or
similar process. Written permission to make a copy or
copies must therefore normally be obtained from the
publisher in advance. It is advisable also to consult the
publisher if in any doubt as to the legality of any
copying which is to be undertaken.

Neither the editors of W. Foulsham & Co. Ltd nor the
author nor the publisher take responsibility for any
possible consequences from any treatment, procedure,
test, exercise, action or application of medication or
preparation by any person reading or following the
information in this book.

This book is meant as a guide only. At all times, if you
have concerns the authors recommend that y ou
contact relevant experts.

*Thank you to Foulsham and Wendy Hobson for their support
and belief in this book, and to Julia Thorley for her editing.*

Printed in Great Britain by Creative Print and Design (Wales), Ebbw Vale

Contents

This book is dedicated to my children, who are a constant source of inspiration to me, and to my fiancée who made this book possible and who has gone through hell with such grace and sensitivity.

Simon Baker

Celebrity endorsements

'Brilliant! About time too!' – Trisha Goddard, host of *Trisha*.

'I wish this book had been around to give to George. Calum had to rely on whatever girlfriend was around at the time. I love this man Simon for making his children a priority. Every man should read this book from 16 to 60.' – Angie Best, former wife of George Best, soccer legend.

Introduction

Going through a divorce can be a tough and gruelling experience. It can be expensive and emotionally and physically draining, and everyone – from your former wife to your children and your friends – will feel the effects of the event. In the UK, for example, hundreds of thousands of couples are divorced and more than 170,000 divorces occur each year, so you are not alone – even though it might feel that way when you are lying awake in the middle of the night missing your children, or trying to figure why you and your ex-wife cannot move on.

The thing to remember is that once the divorce is over and the custody arrangements have been agreed, your new, positive life with your children begins. That is what this book is all about: looking forward and making you the best possible divorced dad you can be. If you are going to be a great divorced dad, you have to look on this next chapter of your life as the chance to create a new life, a new home, a positive, healthy relationship with your children and, all being well, a new working relationship with your former wife.

It is not going to be easy. You will make some mistakes, things may be tight financially and you may have trouble adapting to a new life as a single man with children, but remember that you are not alone and you are doing it for your children.

Whether you are awarded full residency, shared residency or contact rights when you divorce, you still have to create a suitable home and life for your children when they are with you. Whether you see them for just a few days a month or half of every week, you have to be ready to handle a whole range of situations that you and your former wife would have shared. Now it is just you.

For some fathers, creating a new life in a new home with the children when they are with you will come easily; for others it will be harder, and for some of you it will be the biggest challenge of your life! That is why I wrote this book: as a guide to help you answer those questions that have been bugging you; to help you realise there are no stupid questions when it comes to caring for your children; and to help you learn to do the tasks that perhaps your previous partner did and that you were unaware of but you are now responsible for when your children are with you.

You and your children are about to embark on an adventure that, if done correctly, in most cases changes the relationship you have with your children, helping you and them bond at a new and more positive level. Above all, they must know that you love them, care for them and will always be there for them.

It is also important to remember at the outset that while you may feel as though you will be in divorce and post-divorce hell for the rest of your life, you won't. Everyone's experience is different and I have included some worst case scenarios that will not apply to everyone. But take it from me: it is a phase and you will get through it and move on by putting the children first, committing to a businesslike approach with your ex, and learning to be a great divorced dad.

I will be donating a portion of profits from this book to baby charity Tommies. If you are a divorced dad and would like some support, visit my website: www.greatdivorceddad.co.uk or e-mail me at info@greatdivorceddad.co.uk.

Simon Baker
Dad and author

CHAPTER 1

What It Takes to be a Great Divorced Dad

So, where do you start? What goes into making a great divorced dad? Take a look at some of the most important elements of the job you are about to take on:

- Accepting responsibility for the care of your children when they are with you. This is your time to shine and show your children that you can create a safe, secure and loving environment for them.

- Realising that being a great dad when you are married is completely different from being a great divorced dad. When you were married, there were two adults working together. Now there are two adults with different homes and so you have to handle everything in your house by yourself. Don't be unnerved, though; it is all possible and this book will show you how.

- Understanding your children's needs and wants and adequately meeting them is crucial to being a great divorced dad. This means cooking, cleaning, feeding and dressing your children, while still looking after yourself and having a life of your own.

- Making time to be with your children and interacting with them in a positive and proactive way.

- Educating yourself on the child care subjects your former wife used to handle.

- Being able to communicate effectively with your children and discipline them when necessary.

- Not being a 'Disneyland Dad' – a father who thinks parenting is all about over-the-top treats, no routine and junk food solutions to eating.

- Setting in place routines that work for you and your former wife and understanding why routines are critical.

- Learning to communicate with your former wife and putting behind you all the negative emotions that may have come with the divorce.

- Looking after yourself so you can be the positive influence you need to be for your children after the divorce.

- Finding support networks such as dads' playgroups or clubs so you can swap stories and support each other.

- Acknowledging when you don't know something – and knowing whom to turn to for help. Remember: raising children is a constant education and you must never be embarrassed to ask for help.

- Above all, to be a great divorced dad you have to be committed and have staying power. Divorce means that your children's lives as they know them have changed completely. You have to create a new life for them and ensure they do not think they are to blame for the divorce.

So what happens now? How do you make a start to rebuild your life and your children's lives? That's an important question and it all depends on what phase you are at.

Phase 1: just decided to divorce

Your focus must be on five things to be a great divorced dad:

- Telling your children about what is happening in a positive way and ensuring they understand that it is not their fault and that both you and their mother love them.

- Not fighting with your wife in front of the children and shielding them from the anger as much as possible.

- Starting preparations for post-married life with your children. Get a notebook and begin your lists with number one being finding somewhere to live.

- Being prepared for the children's behaviour to change and odd questions to be asked. Now is the time to start learning to go it alone; never use the excuse, 'Ask your mother.'

- Preparing your thoughts about what is important to you and ensuring your children spend the appropriate amount of time with you after the divorce.

Phase 2: going through the divorce

At this stage, you will have told your children and the focus will be more on dealing with the logistics than on the planning. To be a great divorced dad here you must:

- Provide your children with positive reassurance and answer their questions about what is going on so you can ensure that they understand what is going to happen.

- Remain civil to your wife in front of the children and remember that little ears hear everything.

- Start making lists and planning for post divorce. This book will help with those lists and offer guidance on child-raising matters that you might not currently be involved in.

- Ensure your children know you love them and will not leave them and that the divorce is not their fault. Make extra time for them, even if it is just reading a book or going for a walk. They need extra support at this difficult time.

- Remain healthy. Eat well and don't drink too much. There is no shame in seeing a counsellor, if you feel you need to, because it is your children's future that you are fighting for. You can get short-term support if you require it.

Phase 3: the divorce is finalised and it is time to move on

Now that the custody arrangements have been agreed, you and your former partner will have your own homes. Now you must:

● Put in place your post-divorce plan.

● Help your children adapt to their new life between two homes, ensuring they feel secure and loved.

● Make sure that both parents keep open the lines of communication regarding the children. Despite how you feel about your former wife, never speak badly about her around the children and act immediately if the children complain she is speaking negatively about you.

● Be positive for yourself and for your children, and always put their needs first.

● Be prepared for unexpected reactions to the divorce from yourself, your children and friends. Try to deal with them in a positive way.

● Find someone neutral to talk to in the early months.

● Be confident. You and your children are now a new team and Team Dad and Team Mum are not in competition.

● Accept that it is not about winning or who controls the children the most. It is about being the best possible divorced father who is raising happy, healthy and well-adjusted children.

● Be flexible, but ensure that your children stick to a regular routine at your home. Set meal times, bedtimes and household rules provide the security that children need, particularly in the first few months after a divorce is finalised.

TOP TIPS FOR DIVORCED DADS

- Be committed to being a great divorced dad. If necessary, and if the children are old enough, make and sign a divorced dad contract with them laying out your mutual responsibilities. This way, they will feel secure about what to expect in what will be a big change for everyone.
- Identify your strengths and weaknesses and work on the weaknesses.
- Put your children first all the time. Make sure they know the divorce was not their fault and that you are a team.
- Make the time you spend with your children *quality* time, and establish routines and household rules.
- No matter what, try to respect your ex-wife even if she does not respect you. Your children will appreciate it, because she is still their mother. The sooner you both learn mutual respect, the faster you'll recover from the divorce and the better it will be for the children.
- Never be frightened of 'failing' or asking for help. There are hundreds of thousands of divorced dads out there all feeling the same as you. Parenting is something we all learn as we go along.
- Expect the unexpected.
- Look after yourself.
- Be aware that divorce affects people differently. The woman you married is now not the woman you are divorcing, so do not rise to the bait if she tries to cause problems post-divorce and never argue with her in front of the children. Nor must you deliberately upset her. Keep it civil and simple.
- Love your children and be there for them.

Chapter 2

Helping Your Children Adapt to Change

As a great divorced dad, telling your children you are getting divorced and what that means is going to be a difficult conversation to have. Children are incredibly perceptive and if they are living in a house in which parents are going through a divorce they are likely to pick up on a climate of hostility and sadness.

Research has shown that if divorce is imminent, it is best to tell the children as soon as possible, because it:

● Helps them understand what is going on.

● Reinforces that it is not their fault.

● Maintains a level of security.

● Ensures they know that their basic needs are met.

● Helps them understand why there is tension between mum and dad.

● Makes them feel safe and loved.

The more open you are, the less likely it is that behavioural problems will occur.

If your divorce occurs before your children are about two-and-a-half years old, you are lucky in some ways because the children will grow up knowing they have a mum house and a dad house. It is unlikely they will remember mum and dad being together or the arguments.

However, with older children it is critical that you do not allow the children to witness arguments between their parents, as this can be disturbing and upsetting.

Telling the children

No matter how angry each parent is with the other about the separation and divorce, it is critical that you both act responsibly, put aside your differences and tell your children together.

If necessary, have a third party present. This could be a mutual friend who is not taking sides during the divorce, a trusted relative, a mediator, a trained divorce counsellor or perhaps the school counsellor.

As tough as it is when you are going through divorce and custody battles, put your hatred or dislike for each other to one side and work together to tell the children. A parent who suddenly decides to tell the children without consulting the other for some form of win against the other partner is acting irresponsibly and not in the children's best interests.

How to start

Both parents should write down a list of what to say and agree who says what. Remember: this is not a competition and not a way for one parent to win sympathy from the child or children. Once this is decided, get the children together and ensure they are in a place they are comfortable with, such as a favourite room in the house. Remember to use language that is appropriate. Stick to your written plan and use the positive, proactive approach discussed so far.

Ways to explain divorce

There are many ways to explain divorce. However, as this is a sensitive issue it may be worth consulting a divorce mediator before progressing to this phase to ensure that your written plan is appropriate and that you have given sufficient thought to possible reactions.

Under no circumstances should one parent leave it to the other. Both must be present and actively involved.

Choose one of the suggested explanations below and use it consistently. Children need this level of consistency and changing the words you use to explain the divorce causes confusion and stress.

- Mum and dad have come to a decision and we won't be living in the same house any more. It is not your fault.

- Mum and dad have decided not to be married any more and we are going to get divorced. This is not your fault and you will still see us both and we both love you very much.

- Mum and dad are very sorry that we have decided to live in different houses, but it is going to be best for everyone.

- When mum and dad get divorced we won't be getting married to each other again, but you will always be the most important people in the world to us.

- This has nothing to do with you and is not your fault. We will still be your parents and we love you more than ever.

Language to use

The key is to ensure that the language you use reinforces to the children that the divorce is not their fault, they are loved, they will still have a mum and a dad and will have access to them, and that they will be protected and secure. See pages 21–29 for more help on improving post-divorce communication skills.

At all costs, in front of your children you must avoid language that is abrupt, unsettling or that casts blame. Do not say:

- Mum and dad are getting divorced because we do not love each other any more.

- Dad is leaving mum and not coming back.

- Mum and dad are splitting up.

- It is your mother's/father's fault; she/he doesn't love us any more.

Children's reactions

Your children could react in a number of ways, depending on their age and what they have witnessed in the household in terms of arguments or if one of the parents has already moved out. Expect any of the following:

- Impulsive and impatient behaviour.
- Anger at others.
- Oppositional, rebellious, defiant or conduct problems.
- Breaking rules and testing limits.
- Destructive behaviour.
- Anger at self.
- Self-blame or guilt.
- Self-destructive or self-harming behaviour.
- Drug or alcohol use.
- Apathy or failure to accept responsibility.
- Early or increased sexual activity.
- Isolation and withdrawal.
- Suicidal thoughts or behaviour.
- Violent thoughts or behaviour.
- Superficially positive behaviour.

Both parents need to watch for these reactions and act on them. This is a co-parent responsibility and you must put aside the fear that if you raise the issue with your wife she will accuse you of being a bad parent. This is not about you, it is about the children.

These emotions will only last as long as you as a parent allow them to. So as a couple you must:

- Address the tears, anger and bitterness.
- Talk individually and separately to the children but try not to place blame.

- If you get the questions 'Why is this happening?' and 'Whose fault is it?' tell the child it is no one's fault and that sometimes mothers and fathers fall out of love and decide not to be married. Reinforce that you are sorry it is happening and you are available to talk at any time.

- If an affair is involved, often the children will know about it. So your only option is for the person having the affair to admit they have found someone else they love more than their mother/father and that this sometimes happens.

- Above all, answer all the questions. Avoidance causes insecurity and makes the children feel that you are hiding something.

Questions, questions, questions

Once you have told the children the situation, find out how much they know and listen to their questions. Let your child take the lead here and be prepared for the same questions over and over again. This is a child seeking reassurance and clarity. Never give false hope that the divorce may not proceed.

Questions that your children will ask before and after divorce might include:

- Why are you getting/did you get divorced?

- Is it my fault?

- Will you get back together?

- Where will I live?

- Will I still see you both?

- Will we have to move away?

- Will I have to change schools?

- What do I tell my friends?

- Who is going to look after me?

- Does mum divorcing dad mean she is divorcing me?

- If I hadn't been naughty, would you have stayed married?

● If either of you gets married again, does that mean I will have a new mother or father?

● Does living with mum mean I have to love dad less?

In many towns and cities there are support groups for children from divorced families, so talk to the school counsellor and find out if he or she can recommend a group. Also ask older children if they would like to talk to a counsellor or expert on divorce about what is happening. Third-party assurance often helps.

Be open and frank when you answer these questions, but keep your answers simple. Before you start talking about the divorce, decide which parent answers what questions and if a question comes up that is unexpected both answer it in turn. For older children, explain the divorce process and what happens in court (should it come to that).

Communication is critical throughout this process and divorce is confusing for children. Parental anger is felt in the house and often parents try to get the children on their side in the divorce battle. Grow up and stop it. These are your children and you should never use them as weapons in divorce. Respect them and their feelings.

Your children's feelings

Children need to be allowed to express their feelings, even if this means anger, tears and misbehaviour. Encourage older children to write down how they feel and to talk through these issues. Books that tell stories about parents divorcing are useful to read to younger children.

Some children may be relieved their parents are divorcing, while their brother and sister may be devastated. It is crucial you explain these different feelings are equally valid. A child may not understand why mum or dad is relieved about the divorce while the child is sad and hurt. Tell the child that people have different feelings. They must know feelings are neither right nor wrong. For example, you could say, 'I know you are hurt that dad left home and it is OK for you to be sad. But mum and I have been unhappy for a long time.' Tell them that feelings may be different on different days, too.

Children will often think they are the only child in the world to experience divorce and this range of feelings. Ways to deal with this include:

● Finding friends who are divorced but whose children have a happy relationship with both parents. Organise some outings so they can experience a positive divorced family.

● Consider counselling for your children.

● Find out if there are any support groups for divorced parents or children of divorced parents through your local council, school or newspaper. It helps the children to meet other children going through the same thing.

● Most schools teach about different kinds of families, so involve teachers and care-givers in what you are doing.

Basic needs

Your children need to know that whatever is happening between you and your partner, their basic needs will be met. They need to know right from the start that they will:

● Still see both mum and dad. They will have parents who love them and who will be at concerts and school events, and to whom they can talk.

● Have a bedroom at both houses.

● Have someone to read to them at night.

● Have someone to help them with their homework.

● Have someone to make their favourite food.

● Have someone to give them pocket money, buy their clothes and be there for them at any time.

● Continue to have a relationship with both parents and not be asked to take sides.

Permanency of divorce

Some children think their parents will get back together and may misread your or your ex-wife's actions. Signs that they think this may be happening include:

- Constantly asking for the other parent to visit or come to dinner during your time with them.

- Asking to see family photos.

- Making up stories to friends that there is no divorce.

- Simply refusing to accept that the divorce is happening.

If this occurs, first make sure that neither you nor your ex-wife is giving out the wrong message. For example, children might view a reduction in arguments and parents being civil to each other as the divorce being off. Both of you should address the issue with the children and provide comfort and support.

How do children balance relating to two divorced parents?

This is a good question. Your job is to explain the difference between parental love and the love you feel for your child, and to reinforce that it is all right to love mum and dad the same.

After a divorce – and particularly if there has been a court hearing to decide custody – a child's loyalty may split. They may feel caught between the parents. Though the parents may never ask a child to take sides, children can still feel they have to choose one parent over the other. Give them space and time to find what they feel comfortable with.

The key is never to use the children as weapons in the divorce battle. Simple explanations can help: 'Sometimes you may feel guilty for missing mum while you are staying with me. Sometimes you may feel you have to choose whether you love mum more or me more. It is OK to feel all these confused feelings and thoughts. Many children feel that way when their parents get divorced.'

Family divorce meetings

I recommend that two weeks after you first tell the children about the impending divorce you get together again for a family discussion. Ask questions, answer them and, if you feel it would be helpful, have a mediator there. Talk about the children's fears and concerns and don't lie. Even if you hate each other, put those feelings aside for the benefit of the children.

Hold regular conversations with the children as and when they need it. The more involvement they have and the more you address the issues, the easier it should be.

TOP TIPS FOR HELPING CHILDREN TO ADAPT

- Put aside your hatred between yourself and your spouse.
- Put the children first.
- Tell them as soon as possible and prepare beforehand.
- Use a mediator if necessary.
- Ensure your children know that it is not their fault and that they are loved.
- Have regular family divorce discussions.
- Keep your original explanation consistent. Do not change your stories or it will confuse and stress your child.
- Be prepared for any question and any response.
- Don't kid yourself: your children will know something is going on, so be mature and remember that your children are the most important people in the world.
- Never use your children as weapons in the divorce and custody battle. Do not lie to them or try to buy their love.

CHAPTER 3

The Language of Your Post-divorce Life – Keeping It Positive

As a great divorced dad, it is critical that you learn a new language, which I sometimes call 'positive post-divorce speak'. It is aimed at helping you to move on and at making the children feel secure and safe in your home.

I didn't realise I was speaking differently

Before you divorced, you were a family and families are the norm in society. There is a mum, a dad and the children. There is the family home and the parents love each other. However, during divorce, that changes. You start using legal terms, such as custody battle, non-custodial parent, custodial parent, shared residency, access visits, legal home and so forth. There is likely to be anger in the family as the structure breaks down. No matter how much you try not to argue in front of your children, they pick up on the tension and they hear the disagreements.

There could be several months – or even longer – during which your children may hear words and phrases like these on a regular basis: unfit parent; investigation; Form E; CSA; child support; unwanted; uninvolved; aggressive; acrimonious; domestic violence; broken home; shocking father; deliberately withholding money; he hates me and the children; I can't believe she/he broke up our family and had the affair. For children who hear these and other words, their life becomes very confusing.

They may not understand them, they may think one parent wants them to take sides or they may blame themselves.

Positive post-divorce speak

During and after a divorce, it is up to you and your partner to create two homes with no anger or aggression. No matter what the custody arrangements are, you must create a new family structure in which your children have two homes and two families, and feel wanted and loved in both places.

Be aware of the power of language; making sure that you both use positive language can go a huge way to making that happen. That is why it is important that you examine the language you use and commit to using positive language. If you change the way you refer to issues and do it regularly, then you create a more positive atmosphere and focus on your new family life. It sets a good example for the children and they will, in turn, start using the positive terms.

Meeting and greeting

Positive language comes from working towards mutual respect. It is up to you to set a positive example to the children, so when you collect the children from your ex-partner or she collects them from you always say: 'Hello, how are you?' Encourage your children to give their mother a hug or say hello, and then give your ex-partner a quick run down on things she needs to know: if the child has been given medication or if he or she got an award at school or if, for example, he is learning to swim and did a lap of the pool by himself. Always say goodbye and encourage the children to say goodbye, and say, 'I'll see you on Monday' or whatever.

It is possible that in the early stages your ex-partner may ignore and blank you. She may not even come to the door, but just leave it ajar. You should still say, 'Hi, Jane. The children and I are here. I have left their bags on the step and they had a nice weekend.'

Persevere and if necessary write a letter asking her if, for the children's sake, she could please acknowledge your pleasantries. It is critical that you both start being pleasant to each other and saying hello and goodbye for the children's sake. If your ex-wife ignores your hello and goodbye, it sends a negative message to the children that mum doesn't like or respect dad. After all, if a friend or handyman came to the door she would say hello, so why not say it to dad? Similarly, you and your ex-partner encourage your children to say hello to visitors and friends, so parents deserve the same respect.

Childlike behaviour from one former spouse's side is harmful to the children's view of the other parent and is disrespectful.

Positive language

Even between two people who once loved each other enough to create a family, divorce can bring out the worst in each of you. Think before you speak.

Words used during divorce	Positive alternatives
Ex-wife, ex-partner, ex-husband, soon to be ex, that bloody woman, slag, cow.	Children's mum/mother.
Ex-husband, ex-partner, that bastard.	Children's dad/dad.
Marriage failed, breakdown, acrimonious divorce.	The marriage ended.
Matrimonial home.	The children have two homes, one with their mother and one with their father.
Access visit, contact visit.	Spending time at dad's/mum's home, spending time at your other home.
I am divorced and I have children.	I have a family; they live with their mother part of the time and with me the other part.
Broken home, split family.	New family structure, dad's home and mum's home.
Mum's new partner (unmarried).	Partner, co-carer.

Words used during divorce	Positive alternatives
Mum marries.	New husband/step-parent.
Dad's new partner (unmarried).	Partner, co-carer.
Dad marries.	New wife/step-parent.
Mum's new boyfriend.	Mum's new friend or special friend.
Dad's new girlfriend.	Dad's new friend or special friend.
New partner's children by other marriage.	Expanded family, new step-siblings, step-brothers and sisters or co-brothers and sisters.
Describing divorce.	Dad and mum used to love each other but that has changed – they are friends now and love you both very much; you have two new homes with special people in them who love you.
Court orders.	New rules the judge gave us to live by.
Alteration to the orders.	Dad wants to ask the judge if he can spend more time with you.
Adulterous affair.	Mum/dad met someone new when we were married and stopped loving dad/mum, so now we have two new families and you are very lucky.
I have custody.	The children spend more time at my home but they also have a home with their father/mother.

Ex-partner's anger

Some ex-partners remain bitter for a long time after the divorce and try to use the court orders or arrangements to cause hurt. If, for example, the children are with their mother for 20 nights a month and with you for 10, she might delight in saying things like:

- 'They live with me, not him.'

- 'They rarely see him.'

- 'He gets to take them to McDonald's for tea once a week.'

- 'It is detrimental for them to see him for any more days.'

These are negative messages being sent by the mother who is likely to still be deeply upset by the divorce. But don't forget that your children will hear their mother talking to her friends and you talking to yours.

Even if your children only see you for five nights a month, you still provide a home for them to stay, a room, a place for their toys, their clothes – and love.

Positive post-divorce language is not designed to upset your ex-partner, but rather to remove the negative and aggressive language that prolongs bitterness and blame after a divorce. It is also designed to comfort your children, help create a positive new family structure and give them a strong sense of belonging. This is not about winning or losing, but about appreciating your children's need for security, and assistance in moving on to the next positive stage of your lives as a family unit in which the children have two homes.

What if my ex resists or people criticise me for new words?

Yes, this may happen. You start trying to use positive language and your ex blanks you. Your former wife or partner will probably accuse you of trying to sugar-coat reality or even of lying. Others may say that five nights a month doesn't make a home. Your ex-wife might even go into complete denial and even if you have shared custody try to convince the children and her friends and family that she has custody, that her home is the children's home and that yours is just somewhere they stay occasionally.

Do not put up with this; you need to stick to your guns. The language you use is critical to showing people how you feel and whether your view is positive or negative.

Positive post-divorce language:

● Gives security to your children.

● Signals to everyone you are moving on and being proactive.

● Continues the businesslike approach with your ex.

● Provides your children with a more positive vocabulary to use.

If people criticise you, then try responding, 'Thanks for that input. However, I am choosing to use a new positive post-divorce language because it makes our children feel more secure and helps us focus on the future, not the past.'

Making your children's language positive

While times are changing and more and more fathers are being granted shared residency of their children, most divorced families still see the mother spend more nights with the children than the father.

This can change once the children are old enough to decide for themselves who they want to live with. Until then you will find yourself seeing your children less than your ex and you might have to go back to court to alter the orders as the children make their way through nursery to school. This is not unusual; it's called evolution of contact.

However, children often feel they are being denied access to their dad and yours might miss you greatly. It is often hard for young ones to understand why dad is not around all the time, particularly if their mum has a new partner. That means their time with you is precious and you may find they start using negative language about their mother. As a divorced dad to hear your children saying bad things about their mother may make you very happy and be proof the children are unhappy with the current custody arrangements.

However, remember that children between three and six years of age often don't mean what they say. They may say it because they want to make you happy and may be saying the same thing to their mother: 'I don't want to go to dad's.' Or it may truly be how they feel.

Until you are in a position to deal with the situation and alter access arrangements, if necessary, you must not encourage this negative language. As much as it may upset you, remember that you are their father and your ex is their mother; you created these children together and are responsible for looking after them until they are at least 18. You must teach them respect and show that you respect their mother's position in their life.

Negative child language	Explanations to encourage your child to use positive language
'I don't want to go to mum's.'	'Mum loves you very much and misses you. It is your turn to see her. I'll miss you and be thinking about you all the time.'
'I hate mum.'	'We don't hate anyone in this house. Mum loves you very much.'
'I hate mum's boyfriend.'	You should ask why first, as your children could be trying to tell you that something bad is happening and they need your help. If you feel it is just an adverse reaction to a new male in the mother's household, talk to the mother but tell the child. 'I have met Tom and he seems nice. Would you like me to talk to mum? He makes mum happy so try to get to know him a little better for mum's sake.'
'I hate mum's house.'	Ask why, but also say something like, 'Mum has a lovely house that she bought for you and her and it would make her sad if you didn't like it.'

'Can you pick me up after school, not mum?'	If it is a mother pick-up day you'll have to be honest: 'Today is mum's turn to pick you up. She misses you very much and is looking forward to seeing you. I am picking you up on Friday and you can show me some things in your classroom.'
'Mum cries all the time and yells at her new friend'.	Try to get information from the child. If reports like this continue, talk to your lawyer as it could mean your child is being exposed to another relationship breakdown or other negative issues. A good answer might be: 'I'll talk to mum, but make sure you give her a big cuddle when she gets upset because she likes that.'

Using a parenting diary

Keep a diary or spreadsheet of instances of negative child language: what was said and when and how you handled it. You may see a pattern developing that shows your ex-partner isn't coping with the custodial arrangements or that something negative is occurring in her home. If this is the case, you need to act immediately. Try to talk to your ex or, if that doesn't work, perhaps you need to talk to a lawyer and seek an alteration to the orders. You certainly deserve explanations from the mother if you get reports of negative behaviour on her part or the part of her new partner. A mediator is also an excellent option.

It is your job to protect your child, but *never* put words in your child's mouth or make things up. The situation must be handled with care and sensitivity, so also speak to a counsellor. Your child may be acting up because they miss you and are trying to get more attention.

TOP TIPS FOR POSITIVE POST-DIVORCE SPEAK

- Be prepared for criticism from your ex when you start to use positive language.
- Be prepared for her not to respond to your hellos and goodbyes.
- Practise responses out loud explaining your new language.
- Consider a letter explaining why and asking if she could use the new language, too.
- Remember: this is your new family life. Encourage others to join you in the new language that accompanies it and not to continue post-divorce hatred.
- No one can ever take away the fact you are the father. If you lead by example, you will inspire your children and others.
- Set the standard by which you want to be measured. Be businesslike with your ex and do not let her drag you back into fighting and name-calling. It is not good for you or, more importantly, for your children.
- Listen to your children's negative language and respect their mother's position.
- Keep a diary of your children's negative language as it may indicate that their welfare or happiness is in danger and that changes are required.
- No matter how negative your ex-partner is, you and she are responsible for raising your children and you have to make it work. Warring and disrespectful family structures can only harm them.
- Positive language is best; avoid negativity at all costs.

CHAPTER 4

What to Expect from Your Ex-partner and How to Deal with It

Being a great divorced dad means moving on after your divorce, putting your anger behind you and learning to communicate and deal with your ex-wife or ex-partner in a positive fashion for the benefit of your children. This concept is non-negotiable and is critical in creating a positive and nurturing environment for your children.

As we discussed in the earlier chapter your divorce will either have been a bad one, which was acrimonious and cost a fortune in legal fees, or a good one, which was mutually agreed and entailed no custody battle. No matter what type of divorce you experienced, it is time for you as a father to accept responsibility and acknowledge that you now have an ex. So, you must have a plan on how to deal with that.

Firstly, though, you need to identify the type of ex you have: positive or negative.

The positive ex

A positive ex-wife or partner is a godsend for you as a father and for your children:

- Your divorce was agreeable.
- Your child custody arrangements were mutually agreed and both of you are happy with them.

- You have reached a mutually agreeable financial settlement.

- Your ex keeps you informed of all events in your children's life and you keep her informed.

- You visit each other's homes, talk on the phone and attend school and other events with your new partners, giving your children a positive example that both mum and dad love them and have put the bad times behind them. This is critical in ensuring your children don't think they are to blame for the failure of your marriage.

- You have agreed a positive parenting plan (see page 60).

- You are both working on a positive future for yourselves, your new lives and your children.

Moving forward with the positive ex

Planning a future for you and your children with your positive ex is a relatively simple affair. By having both agreed a parenting plan and remained on speaking terms you are in a position to put your children first, share problems and talk regularly.

The thing to remember is to always keep the lines of communication open. That means agreeing how you and your positive ex wish to communicate key issues. These include:

- Having the same routines at both homes, e.g. bedtimes.

- Health and doctor visit information.

- Discipline matters, especially with older children.

- Behaviour issues.

Most positive exes will simply pick up the phone and talk to each other or have a coffee and go over issues. I also suggest that after a child has been with each parent on a contact visit you follow up with an e-mail about any issues you feel need raising. A regular monthly meeting with your ex for an hour, complete with an agenda (see page 43) is also a good idea. Keep a notebook containing details of the agenda and meetings, so you each know who is doing what and what responsibilities each former partner is taking on that month.

It takes work

The relationship with a positive ex needs to be worked at and regularly maintained. To do this, every few months read through the list below and score yourself out of ten. If you answer no to any of the questions, you or your ex need to do some positive ex-maintenance on the relationship.

Positive ex-maintenance checklist

- Are you both keeping up to your side of the custody arrangements?

- Are you both keeping up to your side of the financial settlement or financial payments?

- Are you both keeping each other informed about all aspects of the children's life that you committed to do under the custody agreement and/or parenting plan?

- Are you respecting each other's time with the children?

- Is either of you breaking the orders in any way?

- Are you respecting each other's new life, partner and privacy?

- Are you blaming each other when things go wrong?

- Are you communicating regularly?

- Are you keeping to agreed routines at both homes?

- Are you putting your children's interests first?

If the answer is no to any question, then get out your parenting diary and make a list of why you think this is occurring. The top five reasons for positive ex breakdown are:

- Financial problems.

- New partner or marriage or divorce guilt relapse.

- Major changes in the children's life, such as changing schools.

- Major changes in a parent's life, such as a new job.

- The child or children are going through different phases, especially in the teenage years.

Once you think you understand the reason for the breakdown, work towards fixing it as a matter of urgency. The top five ways to repair a positive ex relationship breakdown are:

- Talk to your ex. Try to discuss the issue rationally and find a solution.

- Nominate a list of solutions to your ex.

- Give your ex space or additional support.

- Encourage the children to be supportive or offer to take them for extra time to give your ex time for a holiday.

- Re-evaluate the parenting plan to take into consideration changed circumstances.

The most three most important things to remember are:

- The children's needs come first.

- Never allow the lines of communication to disintegrate.

- Do not return to the bad old days of drama and blame.

The negative ex

The negative ex is experienced in many break-ups, sometimes for just a short time and sometimes it never ends. Remember: the negative ex can be the wife or the husband.

- Acrimonious and expensive divorce or separation.

- Acrimonious and expensive custody battle.

- Acrimonious financial settlement.

- Continual attempts by your ex to break the court-ordered custody arrangement.

- Your ex fails to keep you informed of or involved with critical information about your children as a way of punishing you, continuing to control you or make you look bad in front of the courts if the custody battle continues.

- She continually barrages you with demands and allegations that upset your new home life.

- She tries to turn the children against you.

- She refuses to negotiate a positive parenting plan.

- She turns your former friends against you.

- She will not communicate with you.

- She makes your life intolerable by trying to force you out of the children's life and constantly criticising you.

- She refuses to allow you access to your children.

- She shows signs of not moving on and still being addicted to divorce anger.

- Her new relationship post-divorce is not working; if yours is, she is jealous or envious.

Moving forward with the negative ex

From the above list, it appears that moving forward and planning a positive future for yourself, your children and the negative ex is a difficult job. You must understand that you are dealing with raw emotion, anger, hatred, guilt and in some cases remorse. This is a minefield of human drama and negotiating it is tough, because in most cases the children are being used as the weaponry.

To deal effectively with the negative ex, you must:

- Always put the children first.

- Refrain from becoming emotional about anything or returning to the pre-divorce drama that no doubt plagued the entire family's life.

- Be rational and avoid being pulled into screaming matches.

- Introduce a businesslike approach.

- Develop a workable method of communication that doesn't involve the children passing messages. You may have to work hard to maintain this.

- Try to understand why your ex is behaving in a negative way without being accused of interfering in her new life.

Why is your ex negative?

It is critical to identify in your own mind why you have a negative ex. It might be because:

- She is unhappy with the divorce settlement and believes she should have been better treated by the courts. Perhaps you served the papers first or she did not get what she wanted.

- She is unhappy with the financial settlement and believes she should have more. This could come out of the blue because new divorce settlements offering wives larger amounts of money are being set by the courts.

- She has been talking to another divorced friend who in her mind has a better deal than she has.

- She is unhappy with the custody arrangements and believes you should have less time with the children.

- She blames you for the breakdown of the marriage and her family life.

- There was domestic violence in the marriage.

- She is suffering guilt because she broke up the family and marriage.

- The cost of the divorce and custody hearing has crippled her financially and she now hates you.

- She dislikes the fact you are still in her life when she has a new partner.

- She believes she knows best and is angry she has to consult you about the health and educational needs of the children.

- She disapproves of your new partner, your new home or your new friends.

- She appears to have a pathological desire to keep you away from your children and constantly pushes the boundaries of your custody arrangements.

- She still wants to control you and have you as a subordinate.

- She is still obsessing about the divorce and going over old ground, issues raised and settled between lawyers or in the courts months ago.

- She is not coping emotionally and fixates on you and the divorce or separation. Many people who suffer relationship breakdowns often suffer depression.

- She is not coping financially.

- She cannot cope or believe the children would want to spend time with you and not her, because 'I'm their mother'.

- She can't cope with the children coming back to her house and telling her what a great time they had with you.

- She is going through divorce grief or divorce addiction.

- Her new relationship is not working out as she expected or has failed.

Think through this list and, if you think it will help, take out your diary and write down the points that you can attribute to your negative ex. If you can attribute five or more of these points to her, it is likely she is in what is known as the off-the-wall phase of post-divorce recovery and is suffering from divorce addiction. This is not a medical term, but is a term often used to describe the often irrational behaviour of a negative ex. By understanding why she is behaving like a divorce addict, you can work more rationally towards dealing with the relationship.

Understanding the off-the-wall phase and divorce addiction

For many couples, acrimonious divorces are lengthy and expensive. They are like a war, with each side firing legal salvos with letters and claims full of bitterness and in some cases false accusations. The aim is a series of wins for either party until the divorce and custody issues are concluded by the courts.

Many people involved in divorce become addicted to this way of living and to the battles that can give their life focus. Although we are dealing with ex-wives here, of course ex-husbands are just as likely to experience divorce addiction.

These feelings can be incredibly intense and if your divorce has taken place over a 12–24-month period, this way of living may become normal. Once everything is settled there are no more of the divorce highs that the divorce addict needs to feel content, so she continues to behave as she did during the divorce, to the detriment of you and the children. This off-the-wall period or divorce addiction is worn like a badge of honour by the sufferer. She becomes a martyr to the divorce. It stops her moving on because she thrives on the drama she creates and it makes her feel whole and happy. Yet it is destroying any ability to move on.

A divorce addict does not realise she is addicted to divorce in the same way an alcoholic feels that a bottle of vodka is normal and does not recognise the addiction. This means that a divorce addict will not work out her emotions in a businesslike or focused way. She will leap from one drama to another, often using lies, innuendo and negative behaviour patterns to keep the drama going, affecting you, your children and your attempts to move on and open up the lines of communication.

Cycling behaviour

You may also find that a negative ex who is a divorce junkie will cycle. This means she will be fine to deal with for a few weeks or even a couple of months and then out of the blue create a drama designed to:

● Make her the centre of attention.

- Wreak havoc on you and your life.

- Remind you of how bad she thinks you are.

- Affect your contact with your children.

- Try and pull you back into her web of divorce addiction.

These cycling periods of ups and downs can be very disturbing, because when things are going well and are on an upward cycle with your ex, you think you and she are making positive steps and moving on: that she is turning from being a negative ex to a positive ex. However, when the downward cycle occurs it leaves you concerned for the welfare of your children, and her personally shocked, bereft, scared and angry.

Dealing with divorce addiction

The first thing to remember is that in a negative ex situation you may already have little or no means of communication with her. Even if you were to speak to her about a possible divorce addiction or her being in an off-the-wall period, it would have an even worse effect and create even more problems for you and the children.

However, you cannot ignore this behaviour. You must do something because of the effect it will have on your children and their relationship with you and your ex-wife. The key is trying to reopen the lines of communication using every possible method at your disposal. You could:

- Seek counselling yourself. Often talking to a professional counsellor about what you have been through and your wife's behaviour will assist in providing you with an independent sounding board.

- Talk to your ex-wife's new partner. Sometimes the new partner is willing to be an intermediary and you need to reach out and see if this is possible. Be careful when you do this because their commitment is not to you but their new partner, your ex, and it could backfire.

- Suggest mediation, especially if you are still having to return to court over custody issues. You can ask for the judge to order court-appointed mediation with an officer of the Children and Family Court Advisory Service (CAFCAS) who will meet you both separately and then together over a period of time with the aim of working out how to improve communication and put the children's interests first.

Another option is to change the way you deal with your ex and adopt what I call the business ex approach. This is one of the most proactive things you can do for yourself, your children and your ex, particularly because its focus is on neutral communication. But first it is important to understand why you need to do this.

Good familiarity

When you were married, you had what is called good familiarity. You shared an emotional, sexual and family relationship. You built a life and a home together. You shared a life and that life was full of good familiarity; the familiarity was positive and used for good and positive things.

Bad familiarity

When you decide to divorce, the good familiarity of marriage is replaced with bad familiarity. Your positive emotional, sexual and family intimacies are replaced with feelings of anger and hatred. Your entire life is deconstructed. Now instead of using your familiarity for good, it is used for negative purposes, and your ex uses it to find weaknesses.

Unless you have a positive ex, this bad familiarity quickly becomes the basis for one or both of you becoming divorce addicts and living in a permanent off-the-wall phase. Bad familiarity is bad not only for you but also for your children. The children pick up on mum and dad's bad feelings. Often they feel they cannot share experiences at dad's home with mum or the reverse. It also creates a negative climate for joint events such as school sports days and plays.

If you find that your ex-wife has become a divorce addict and is trapped in this bad familiarity lifestyle, you need to take charge using the business ex approach.

Taking charge

To take charge, you have to understand you had good familiarity during your marriage that changed to bad familiarity during the divorce. Now with a business ex approach you will change that to a business familiarity, with the children being your core business, with the hope that one day this may grow into friendship or mutual respect.

Your goals are:

● To break the bad familiarity.

● To stop the off-the-wall phase.

● To help stop your ex-wife's divorce addiction affecting you and your children.

● To help her see there is a better way of moving forward.

● To create business familiarity.

● To find a way to communicate effectively with your ex.

The best thing is to think of yourself and your ex as business executives whose core business is the children you share. Think of how you behave in the workplace and the way you treat your colleagues, how you communicate with them, how you respect them and their space, how you prepare for and hold meetings, and you will have the core elements of how you are going to start dealing with your ex-wife.

You will probably find this tough because you will have to learn a new way of communicating with your ex and of treating her and the situation, and you might be criticised by her for your new methods. You will have to learn to leave your emotional baggage to one side.

The thing to remember is that you are taking the lead. You are implementing a positive, businesslike plan to help yourself, your ex and, most importantly, your children live better lives and communicate with each other. Businesslike does not mean cold-hearted; it means aiming for mutual respect.

Getting started

This is the tough first step. It requires tact, empathy and courage. Using your parenting diary, make a list of all the reasons why you believe your ex is a divorce addict and why your relationship with her is in the bad familiarity phase. Then write the reasons you want this to change.

Next put your thoughts in a letter to her. If you are still communicating via solicitors either have your solicitor send the letter or do it yourself and send a copy to your solicitor.

The key is to be businesslike. Set out a clear plan, make no accusations and remain unemotional. Below is a sample letter. Be aware that every relationship is different and this is only an example meant to guide you on making your first step towards a business ex relationship. The letter is usually best written after you have had a communication from your ex about your children.

Dear Kim,

Thank you for the last phone call about John.

I have been giving a great deal of consideration to how we can work in a more positive way when dealing with matters relating to our son. I am sure you will agree he is our most important priority, and in recent weeks matters relating to the past have been dragged up and there have been some emotional times for us all. I would like to suggest we try a new method of dealing with each other and approach each other on a more businesslike level when it comes to our son.

I propose we do the following:

Communication
If you feel you cannot speak to me on the phone, we agree to e-mail each other once a week on a certain day with an update as to our son's weekly activities and any issues relating to him. I suggest that we e-mail each other when other issues need dealing with or, if it is a simple question, text each other. We keep our communications clear and concise. If you feel the necessity, I am happy to have you copy in a third party – your lawyer or perhaps mediator – who can ensure we both keep to the agreed systems.

Handovers
We agree that when we have handovers we are civil to each other, say hello and ask the other how they are and set a positive example for our son. If there are any negative matters that need discussing, we do so via e-mail, not at handover, because he can be affected by arguing.

Other matters
If we e-mail each other about matters, we commit to replying to the e-mail within 48 hours.

We recommit to abide explicitly by the custody arrangements governing our son and keep each other correctly informed as to all health, education and welfare matters.

We meet once a month for half an hour to discuss major issues relating to our son with each to suggest an agenda in advance. I suggest we do this with a mediator present whom we are both happy with.

We e-mail each other after our son has returned to each home about issues such as clothes he didn't come back with, homework that needs completing, etc.

We keep our communications brief, to the point and specific.

We do not ask our son to pass on messages, nor do we speak badly to him of his other parent.

The rest of the letter can then address specifics relating to your personal situation. For example, you could suggest a six-monthly schedule for who is responsible for what relating to your son, such as: doctor's check-ups; dental check-ups; specialist check-ups; transport to sporting events; school admission forms; special school projects; music lessons; and sports lessons.

Each parent commits to take responsibility for a certain number of things and in return agrees to notify the other of all upcoming appointments, times and results.

Businesslike formal courtesies

Treat your wife as you would a colleague at work in verbal, letter and phone form. Be clear, concise and always enquire if she has the time to discuss a matter before launching in. Above all, remain consistent. For example, at handover even if your ex never says hello, make sure you do. Set a good example.

Focus on the business at hand

In any written correspondence, be clear and concise about the key message. Do not drag up old history or cloud your letter or e-mail with emotion. For phone calls, write a list of the key points you have to make. If the ex drags up an old problem simply say, 'I would like to stick to talking about [the doctor's appointment, music lesson, whatever] as I would like to focus on the matter relating to our son.'

Set out an agenda for meetings

Like any business meetings, write an agenda, e-mail it to your ex, ask for her input and stick to the agenda. Again, do not be sidetracked by emotion or past history. Business ground rules apply at this meeting. After the sessions, follow up with a letter or e-mail to put in writing what was discussed. It formalises things and you can refer back to your paper trail should the matter come up again.

Do not try to ambush your ex by introducing new items at the last minute. This is not businesslike.

Make no assumptions

Do not assume that your ex-wife knows something relating to an issue. Be clear, take nothing for granted and be concise when laying out the necessary key points of an issue or problem.

Common problems and goals

Common problems and goals that you and your ex will have to deal with are explored throughout this chapter. It is critical that when these come up you deal with them in a businesslike manner via letter, e-mail or mediation. In the early days after a divorce, often both partners are too scared to admit they may be having a problem with their child, for example, enforcing bedtime, for fear that the other party will accuse them of being a bad parent. Adopt a businesslike approach and simply ask your ex for feedback and her thoughts.

Allow no improper confrontations

Do not ambush your ex at meetings or in letters by going off the wall yourself or ignoring your own business rules. Prevent your ex from doing the same by remaining calm and keeping to the agenda of meetings. If she raises fresh allegations in letters, reply to them in a businesslike, proactive way, backed up by supportive evidence.

Be unemotional, calm and rational

Keep your correspondence businesslike. Reread all letters and ask yourself: if I sent this to a work colleague, would they find it acceptable? Better still, ask someone you trust to read the letter and suggest alterations. Do not rise to acts of intimidation. For example, if you receive a nasty text do not reply. Ignore it. Be professional and in your next correspondence request that all texts be kept professional. Your ex is more likely to regret an ill-judged text if you do not react.

Keep information about your personal life to a minimum

Don't talk about your post-divorce personal life in front of your ex unless it concerns your child. It can inflame and create jealousy. If there is a major change in your life, such as a new partner or pregnancy, inform her in writing in a businesslike way and discuss how you are going to inform your other children.

Ask your friends and relatives to adopt a businesslike approach

This is important. Tell your friends and relatives your plan and ask for their support. Tell them your goal is to create a more proactive environment for everyone. Relatives might try to step in to defend you, but that can often make things worse and keep the battles raging.

Consider detailed contracts and agreements

During the early stages of this businesslike approach, for issues not set out in the court orders relating to custody, when you agree something important then put it in writing and have both parties sign it. For example, if you have family coming to visit and you have asked your ex for some of her days and she agrees, ask her to sign a letter about it or do the same when agreeing a holiday. Set it out something like this:

> *I, John Smith, and I, Wendy Jones, agree that John can take our son Raymond on holiday to Hawaii from the 10 June to the 20 June.*   *Signed.*

This example could be used when it is agreed that one parent has an extra day contact for a special event:

> *I, John Smith agree to allow Wendy Jones to have Raymond for an extra weekend on 5 May so he can see his maternal grandparents. In return, I will have an additional weekend normally assigned to Wendy on 2 June.*   *Signed.*

Keep all agreements in your diary.

TOP TIPS FOR GOOD COMMUNICATION

- Remember that communication is key and at all costs you must work to keep open positive communication lines for the benefit of your children.
- Identify whether you have a positive or a negative ex.
- Make no assumptions and be as aware of your ex's sensitivities as you hope she will be of yours.
- If you have a negative ex, identify what the reasons are for this and aim to address them. Be aware of how her behaviour can affect you and your children.

- Adopt a businesslike approach to dealings with a negative ex and if necessary involve a third party, such as a lawyer or mediator.
- Aim for mutual respect or at least some form of communication that allows both of you to parent your children properly.
- Look at yourself and see if you are behaving as a negative ex. Stop any such behaviour.
- With a negative ex, keep contact to a minimum and make sure it is concise, informative and unemotional.
- If your divorce was acrimonious, ensure you copy in your lawyers on all correspondence.
- Keep a detailed diary in case you need to return to court.
- Talk to your children and ensure they are OK.
- Talk to the new partner about the situation, but be careful not to ask them to take on too much.
- Constantly assess yourself and see if you have done something to trigger the problem. If you have, address it immediately.
- Keep your children to their routine at your home. This is critical; you must be their rock if your ex is a divorce addict or behaving in a negative way.
- Remember: it takes two people to make a baby and after divorce those two people must still be committed to caring for the child.
- Do not be tempted to react to provocation.
- Stay in control; stay businesslike.

CHAPTER 5

Making a Home for Your Children at Your House

No matter what residency arrangement is negotiated, your children now have two homes, one with mum and one with dad, and it is up to you as their father to understand the full ramifications of this.

When I divorced with shared residency, I had to move to a different town as part of the new arrangement. My ex-wife and I each bought a new home. What was critical to me was my children understood they had two homes and that at my house they had their own room, their own space and their own belongings. I adhered strictly to a policy of referring to dad's house and mum's house, thus ensuring that the children knew they had two homes in which they could feel safe at all times, and that they didn't have to choose sides.

As a father, you should remember that the time a child spends at each home does not matter; it is the sense of belonging that is critical. Even if you only see your children four nights a month, they must know and feel that they belong at your house and that it is a home for them, as well.

Your new home

Let's face it: post-divorce you might be paying maintenance to your ex and payments for your children, and you might find that your financial circumstances mean that you can only afford a one-bedroom flat or house (and of course, the same could be true of your ex).

If your children are old enough to understand, you should explain why you and they have had to move to a smaller property. Tell them why the former main family home has been sold. They might question why their new room is different or smaller or needs to be shared with someone else. Always be straight with your children and answer their questions honestly. Be realistic and don't make promises you cannot keep, but make sure they feel secure.

No matter how small your new home, always ensure that your children have a section of the house or flat that is theirs. Even just a drawer, a cupboard or a toy box will help to show your children that they have been considered.

Older children can be invited to view potential new homes. This will give them a greater sense of control during a time when divorce makes them feel out of control, and shows them that you value their opinion. If feasible, you could even let them decide which room is theirs.

Celebrate the first time they stay as their official moving into their new home with a small party.

Only one bedroom

Even if your new home has only one bedroom, there are things you can do to make it welcoming for your children. They must never feel they are an intrusion or an afterthought because they may not enjoy staying with you if they feel uncomfortable.

- Have a fold-out bed for them and give them space to store it and the bedding. If possible, let them be involved in the purchase. Alternatively, let them sleep in your room and you sleep on the sofa; this demonstrates how important they are to you.

- Give them part of your chest of drawers and cupboard to store the things they leave with you.

- Ensure they have their own named hangers for coats at the door and places to store their outside boots. Even something as small as this makes a child feel wanted.

- Make space in the bathroom cabinet for their toothbrushes, toiletries and bath toys.

- Space is especially vital for teenagers. They are studying and also going through a difficult phase, so offering them your room when they are with you is helpful.

Your children's rooms

If you can afford a home with a room for each of your children, and if they are old enough, let them be involved in decorating it. Teenagers could be given a budget for the decoration. Even younger children aged between two and five can help you decorate by choosing a special rug or toy or helping put up posters or cartoon wall decorations. This will give them a sense of ownership and will help ease them through the transition from everyone living as a family to having two homes.

Negotiate colour schemes. For younger children, try to use similar colours to the room they had in their family house. Some might want duplicate items in both households: for example, the same duvet cover, blanket or lamp. Talk to them about it and if you have a positive relationship with their mother discuss it as a group.

Do not use children's rooms as dumping grounds for spare stuff and boxes of unpacked household items. It must be clear of your junk; otherwise your children will think they are sleeping in a store room.

Respect your children's space. Knock before you enter and show them you want this to be their special place at the home they share with you.

Basic checklist for your children's room

In the past, many men would have allowed their wives or girlfriends to play a key role in buying things for the house and setting it up or have worked as a team putting a house together. Now this is your responsibility, so the following checklist might help you through the process:

- Cot, toddler bed or normal single bed and mattress – if space is at a premium a travel cot can be used for toddlers.

- Sheets (two sets).

- Duvet.

- Duvet cover (two).

- Plastic under sheet (two for younger children in case of leaking nappies or bed wetting).

- Pillow (two).

- Pillow case (four).

- Bed lamp or night light.

- Chest of drawers.

- Cupboard.

- Toy box, non-lockable and with a slow, safety collapsing lid.

- Desk, lamp and chair for older children to encourage study.

- Bookshelf.

- Bin.

- Curtains or blinds and blackout curtains for younger children.

- Favourite picture or poster from old family home.

- Framed pictures of the children with you.

- Changing table for a baby.

Many stores sell complete kits of bedding with matching curtains featuring favourite cartoon characters, heroes or colours, which can be a relatively cheap option.

Additional items and room decoration

It will add to your child's sense of belonging if you let them help you decorate the room. For example, I bought peel-on-peel-off Barbie and Action Man stickers for my three-year-olds to put around their beds and let them put them on themselves. They don't take the paint off and the children can move them around.

Teenagers will want more involvement to create their own personal space so let them help with choosing flooring, colour schemes and furnishings, and give them a budget. You will have to deal with the issue of computers, CD players, DVD players and televisions yourself, depending on what you can afford and whether or not you want them in the child's room.

Sometimes older children may take advantage of the two-home situation by saying they have something at their mother's house and want the same thing at your house. You should resist the plea of, 'But we have one at mum's house!' Try talking to your ex to determine whether there is general agreement that the same item is needed at both homes.

Remember: this is your house and your rules apply. Do not try to buy your children's love by giving them everything they want. Budgeting and earning items for the room by good behaviour are excellent lessons to learn.

Stick to your budget

Before you start buying, decide on a budget and make a list of all the things you need. Shop around and also arrange with your ex-wife to split linen and duvets, so at least the children have some familiar items. Don't get into debt because you feel guilty that you can no longer give your children everything they want. It may take time to get your finances back on track but if you don't overspend and slowly build up items, you will steadily return to a more stable financial position. Remember: you have to provide suitable accommodation for your children, even if you only see them one weekend a month.

Hallway

Remember: this is a home for you and the children, so welcome them in the hallway:

- Hooks at child's level for coats and a box for fleeces.

- Boot storage area for children.

- Display board for their artwork.

- Identifiable storage area for school or nursery bags.

- Reachable doorbell for all sizes of small people.

Living room

You will need items in the lounge or reception room of your home for your children that make it feel more personal to them. As well as the usual equipment, you might want to consider:

- Toddler chairs (for good posture) for watching TV.

- High chair or booster seats for the dinner table.

- Bean bag – great for play.

- Toy box with suitable toys with safety lid.

- Supply of educational DVDs and books.

- Storage area for children's DVDs, CDs and books.

Ensure that somewhere there is a photo of their mother – perhaps in an album or in their room. No matter how acrimonious your divorce, the children need to feel they can talk about their mother. Ideally there should be a photo of you in their mother's house.

Bathroom

Your children's bathroom needs will vary dependent on age. You are likely to need:

- Portable bath for a small baby.

- Steps for reaching the toilet and sink.

- Potty and potty toilet seat. You can buy a fantastic musical throne potty that plays music when a child sits down. They are great for encouraging a toddler to try toileting.

- Children's shampoo and conditioner.

- A mild, unscented soap.

- Bath toys.

- Flannels (four for a baby or toddler).

- Sponges.

- Bubble bath.

- Towels (three per child).

- Beach or swim towel for holidays or swim lessons.

- Children's toothpaste – small children should never use adult toothpaste.

- Children's toothbrush – change every three months.

- Children's hair brush – adult brushes can be too harsh.

- Non-slip safety mat for the bath or shower.

- Home medical kit.

- Laundry baskets (see page 55).

Outside

It is important when your children are with you that they don't spend all day on computers or watching television, so if possible make your outside area child friendly:

- Covered area for play – consider a retractable awning, gazebo or large umbrella.

- For toddlers and young children a small sandpit – I recommend the ones that are on legs.

- Slide made by reputable manufacturer.

- A Wendy House and/or play tent.

- Fenced garden area with lockable gate or nearby safe park.

- If you have toddlers or children through to the age of six, buy them a tricycle with a parent handle on them so it replaces the buggy and is more fun.

- For older children mini trampolines and bikes for teenagers, but ensure you have safe storage.

- Outdoor table and chairs – picnics in your own garden are just as much fun as going to the park.

- Cardboard boxes – if you get any big boxes, keep them, because children love to play with them both inside and outside: and it saves you a fortune buying a Wendy House! When the children get sick of the boxes, recycle them.

- Buggy with buggy board for toddlers.

- Nappy bag – which then becomes a bag for toddler clothes and other items on family outings. Make sure it has a separate waterproof section for soiled clothes and nappies.

Once the house is set up

You should hold a small party to celebrate the first time the children officially move into and stay at your house. Invite their friends around and have a celebration tea with games. Let them show their new home to their friends so they, too, are familiar with the new home and location.

It is important that your children are familiar with the area you live. Even children from the age of three will recognise streets close to 'dad's house'. When you get in the car, ask them 'Where are we going?' and you will get the response, 'Dad's house!' This is part of children being aware of their local area.

For older children, ensure they learn their address, know where the park is, the shops and the safe place to cross the road, ride bikes and skateboards and catch buses. Also set boundaries for places that are off limits.

Older children should be given strict rules about what they can and cannot do in their rooms and what responsibilities they have. In return, respect your children's privacy.

Keep it safe

Make sure that your children know they can leave things at your house and that you will keep them safe. This is part of a child wanting to leave their mark on the house and their way of saying they acknowledge that this is their home and they will be coming back.

You *must* keep the item so that when the child comes back to your house you can give it back. Never lose it; it reduces trust.

Laundry baskets

Children will have clothes they come to you in that they need to go back to their mother in. They will also have clothes they move between two houses, as well as clothes that stay at dad's house. With this in mind, it is a good idea to have two laundry baskets.

I can't count the number of times I have scrambled through a load of washing trying to find my children's clothes from their mother's house. So I sorted this out with having two washing baskets. When the children take the clothes off, I put the ones to go back to their mother in 'mum's basket'. No mix-ups and no bother and a real time-saver for any hard-working dad! It also ensures the children's favourite clothes or school uniforms are always in the right place.

This is not only courteous but also prevents arguments and any accusations that clothes have not been sent back. Make sure the children know which bag is which and why they need to be careful. Perhaps you could put a picture of mum on her bag.

Similarly, make your child responsible for cleaning rugby, soccer and other sports shoes, with your help, if necessary. Try to ensure the same policy is used at your ex-wife's house.

Household safety

Make sure your new home is safe and child friendly:

- Coffee tables and other furniture with no sharp edges or that have been safety protected.

- Stair and door gates to keep toddlers in rooms and off stairs.

- Covers to keep little fingers out of electrical sockets.

- Protective door latches to stop toddlers opening cupboard doors.

- Door alarms that can be set to tell you if a toddler has gone into an out-of-bounds area. I have one on the freezer to tell me when the children have opened it and not shut it and one on the front door to tell me if they have opened the front door without permission.

- Protective film on glass doors or consider replacing glass doors with anti-shatter, childproof glass.

- Non-slip guards under loose mats.

Can mum see my room?

No matter what age, children will be proud of special things and this includes their rooms. When your children start living between two homes they may ask if their mum can see their new room or something else in your home.

This is a question that needs to be handled carefully. You may wish to protect your privacy if it has been a particularly acrimonious split. However, if you get on with your ex and you can be sure that if she visits the house she won't criticise, then consider allowing her to visit to grant the child's request.

If there is still acrimony between you and your ex-wife consider taking some photographs of your child in their room they can show their mum and friends. It is a compromise, but one that shows your child you have a level of flexibility and put their needs first.

However, make sure your ex understands that the photos have been taken for the child's benefit or she might mistake the gesture as you showing off.

If your ex asks to see your home and the children's room and you are having difficulties with her, it might be best not to allow her in. Tell her you will respect her privacy and that she must respect yours. The reason for this is that she is likely to find fault with your home.

If it comes up in legal letters, offer a third party to view the property, which will protect your privacy. If it is in the court orders that she can inspect your home, you could and should request a reciprocal arrangement. Discuss this with your lawyer and, again, consider a third-party presence.

Your new home is part of you building a new family life with your children and, most importantly, moving on. Protect that concept as much as possible and ensure your ex understands that in return you will respect her new lifestyle.

TOP TIPS FOR MAKING A NEW HOME FOR YOUR CHILDREN

- Within your budget, buy or rent a property with space to give the children a sense of belonging and security.
- Negotiate with your ex to split the children's toys, furniture and other items so some of their favourites are at mum's house and dad's house.
- Young children, under the age of five need and like consistency so if possible keep consistency with the family home – for example, buy the same night light that mum has taken to her new home for them.
- Give older children a budget to decorate their room, or to buy new toiletries that stay at your house. Within reason, let them help to create their new second home.
- Your children's involvement is crucial, so ensure you ask for their input. They should know this is their other home, no matter how big or small it is.
- Allow them to leave things at your house. It is their way of saying: 'I am your child and I belong here, too.'
- Ensure your house is child safe.
- Don't let a sense of guilt lead you to spoil the children with material possessions.
- Regularly use the checklist for items you need to replace or add as the children grow.
- Respect older children's privacy.
- Ensure your home is decorated in a way that makes the children feel they belong.
- Keep a photo of your ex in an album so the children can see it if they wish to.
- Stick to your budget.

CHAPTER 6

Establishing a Routine at Your House

Routine is critical to any child's life. It helps a child feel secure, it helps run a household efficiently and it creates critical guidelines that will help your child be a well-adjusted, well-mannered and well-behaved person. After divorce, routine is even more critical. As a great divorced dad, you must realise that a similar routine at both new homes will make the post-divorce adjustment easier for you and your child and make them feel more secure about the new arrangements.

Especially for young children, routine:

- Sets up the way the day is run.

- Sets limitations and boundaries.

- Provides critical guidelines and ground rules for older children, helping them know what you consider negative and positive behaviour.

- Aids proper behaviour and discourages bad behaviour or developmental problems.

- Allows a household to run efficiently – but beware that too much rigidity has the same effect as no routine at all.

- Gives children a lifelong ability to live in a structured manner.

- Makes a child feel safe and loved. If things happen at the same time on a regular basis, there is no need to fear that something is wrong.

After divorce and the upheaval it causes, it is critical that you stick to the routine of the child staying at each parent's on the same days each week, and that includes being dropped off and collected at the same time. From an early age, children's expectations in a well-run household become finely tuned. When things fall out of sync, children can become concerned or confused. Often fathers see their children less than mothers do, and are accused of letting the child run riot at their home. You must avoid this at all costs. No matter how much you miss your children, spoiling them and deviating from the routine does not help anyone.

Having said that, circumstances sometimes dictate that a routine has to be altered, which is fine so long as it has been properly prepared for. For example, you and your ex can agree to alter contact arrangements as long as the children are told in an appropriate manner (and, when they are old enough, their agreement sought). If their mum is going on holiday, tell the children in advance that you will care for them. If you don't, you are being unfair. Rules will have to be adapted as the children grow; be prepared for an emotional roller-coaster at such times.

Positive routine

Numerous studies prove that no matter what the setting, positive routines should incorporate:

- Basic needs, such as meal times, and structured tasks, such as tidying rooms, making the beds and setting the table.

- A variety of interesting activities, depending on age. This might mean walks, swimming and sport, or organised clubs such as Brownies or football training.

- Transition time from one parent's house to the other.

- Rest time.

Before discussing routine at your house, we need to look at whether you are co-parenting your children or parallel parenting your children in conjunction with your ex-wife.

Co-parenting

This occurs after divorce when parents have a good relationship and can openly discuss issues. Also, they might come together for special family events. Co-parenting often involves having agreed a written co-parenting plan, having discussed which parent should deal with certain specific issues including education, child handovers, bedtime and meal times, so that routines remain basically the same at each parent's house. This way there is minimum disruption for your children, and lessening in the likelihood of behaviour problems.

Whether your divorce is resolved through solicitors or the courts, I recommend that you and your ex-wife work out a parenting plan. Then, should it come to a custody battle, you will be able to show that you have given your post-divorce life some thought. You might also wish to consider setting up a mediation fund, so that there is money set aside to pay for help should you need it in that difficult first year. Alternatively, the court might be able to appoint a free mediator to assist you.

Parallel parenting

This is more likely to be the parenting style being experienced in the first few years after divorce. Each parent usually thinks his style is the only way to parent and is often quite critical of the other. For example, your ex-wife may not tell you what time she usually puts the children to bed or gives them their meals, which can cause problems for you and upset the children.

What you have to do is to suggest a co-parenting plan to your ex, perhaps in the presence of a third party. This will give you the opportunity to sit down together to work out a proper co-parenting plan and discuss issues without arguing.

The goal is to reduce the level of conflict and make sure that the tasks of parenting are accomplished by both parents in the same routine. It is important that both parents agree which person is responsible for which of the various parenting tasks. To do this you might need the help and support of a neutral decision-maker or even the courts. The aim is to ensure that parents communicate with each other with less conflict.

Routine at your house

So how do you establish a positive parenting routine at your house? This is determined by the child's age and what you and your ex-wife have agreed.

If the routine the children had at your marital home worked, then it should continue at both of the new homes. Don't fix something that isn't broken. Nor should you think that by giving the children more freedom it will help them recover from the divorce and love you more. It won't; in fact, it could even make things worse.

If you have agreed a parenting plan, put it in writing and ensure that you and your ex-wife sign off on it. If you didn't, write to your ex-wife (see page 41 for a businesslike letter approach) suggesting a routine and ask for her feedback. Ensure you copy in your lawyer and/or mediator, if appropriate. A suggested routine is given below.

Basic routine for all children

	Jane	Tom
Wake-up time		
Breakfast time		
Play time or nursery		
Lunch time		
Nap time		
Snack time		
Play time		
TV time		
Dinner time		
Bath time		
Book reading time		
Bedtime		
Other		

Next to each point write a time or a comment. Depending on the children's age, show them the routine and draw up a reward chart that allows them to collect stars for following it.

Even with children under 12 months old, you and your ex should agree a routine that includes the specifics of sleeping, play time and eating. From one to four years of age, ongoing changes to an agreed routine will include the amount of nap time they need, perhaps extension to nursery attendance, play dates with their friends and bedtime and meal time alteration. They might also start lessons such as ballet or sport, which will also need including.

I have a big year planner in the kitchen that lists every day of the year and I use coloured dots to identify when my children are with me, when there are holidays and so on (see page 63).

A schedule like this means you can both have a copy and there is no confusion. You can also provide it to the nursery or other essential care-givers. It is particularly useful if your ex is trying to cause you problems by breaching agreements. You have set out the fortnightly routine as agreed with your ex in your businesslike dealings or as laid out by the courts.

Creating a routine for your toddler

The top 10 'must-do' elements of a toddler's routine are:

- Get them up on time and to bed on time.

- Give them their meals on time.

- Allow free play.

- Play a number of different games with them.

- Take them out for fresh air to the park or in the garden.

- Take them out socialising.

- Read to them.

- Encourage them.

- Give your child quality attention time.

- Stick to your routine and provide your child with security.

John's fortnightly schedule

Current week	Location	Delivered by and time	Collection by and time
Monday	Nursery	Mother deliver by 9 am	Mother collect at 3.30 pm, overnight with mother
Tuesday	Day with mother	Day with mother	Overnight with mother
Wednesday	Nursery	Mother deliver by 9 am	Father collect 3.30 pm, overnight with father
Thursday	Day with father	Day with father	Return to mother 7 pm
Friday	Nursery	Mother deliver by 9 am	Father collect at 3.30 pm, weekend with father
Weekend			
Monday	Nursery	Mother deliver by 9 am	Mother collect at 3.30 pm, overnight with mother
Tuesday	Day with mother	Day with mother	Overnight with mother
Wednesday	Nursery	Mother deliver by 9 am	Father collect 3.30 pm, overnight with father
Thursday	Day with father	Day with father	Return to mother 7 pm
Friday	Nursery	Mother deliver by 9 am	Mother collect at 3.30 pm, weekend with mother

So how do you achieve this?

Plan tasks such as major grocery shopping, laundry and house cleaning for times when you do not have the children with you. This gives you more time with them. Make a list of all the things you need to do in the day when the children are with you. Then the night before, put things ready for the morning and make sure you are awake before your toddler.

Try to create a wake-up routine. This might be:

- Toddler wakes.

- Cuddles with dad.

- Then uses the toilet, washes their hands, cleans their teeth.

- Gets dressed.

Keep a chart and give the child a sticker when they do these things. Encourage them to be independent.

Set a time for breakfast – 8–8.30am is good – and ensure you involve your toddler with preparing it. I advise no TV until after breakfast, because there is a tendency for youngsters to become involved in a programme and not want to eat. Eat breakfast together and talk about the day ahead. Get your child to help clear away after breakfast, then allow some free time play or TV.

I divide my children's toys up into boxes so they have their puzzles in one, train set in another, play dough in another, etc. We discuss which box we want to play with and have Tidy Up Time afterwards. Then we choose another box. In your diary, keep a record of what you do each day, so you can alternate what toys are played with, and vary what TV programmes or DVDs they watch.

Aim for a snack at around 10am, then go out for a walk or to the park, then back home for more play.

Involve your children in preparing the lunch and eat together, again with no TV or DVD playing. Aim for an afternoon nap after lunch followed by more play, but this time something more structured, perhaps involving crafts. Then have an afternoon outing or play in the garden

Have dinner at around 5.30pm, then give your child a bath. Once he is in his pyjamas, have some quiet time with a book and a cuddle. Aim for bedtime at 7pm.

Bedtime is the hardest part of most toddlers' routines. Many will try and push the boundaries continually and there will be tears. Stick to your guns and your routine. Ensure your toddler has his favourite toy, blanket and night light. Given them a count down to bedtime, giving a ten-minute warning, and stick to it.

Take them into their bed and lay them down, perhaps read to them and then say good night and leave the room. You must not allow them to come running out. Be strong and say no and put them back into bed and close the door. This may go on for some time but eventually they will fall asleep.

Routine for children 5 to 12 years old

Routine changes dramatically for this group of children, principally because from about 9am until 3.30pm they will be at school. This may mean getting up earlier, going to bed earlier and cutting back TV time. You'll have to factor in events such as clubs, visiting friends, music lessons and after-school events, as well as homework that requires your participation.

However, the daily routine will be slightly easier to control. It should run like this:

● Prepare school clothes and bags the night before.

● Wake before your children and prepare breakfast.

● Children up, shower, clean teeth and dressed for school.

● 9am Children at school.

● 3.30pm Collect from school.

● Afternoon can include homework, free play, structured play, out-of-school sports or music lessons, TV watching and computer time.

● 6.30pm Dinner time with everyone present. Involve children in cooking or cleaning up afterwards.

● Then family time, bath time and bedtime.

Problems with this routine differ from those you might have with a toddler. Children may be tired when they first start school. Alternatively, if they have been in full-time nursery care they will have extra energy, because school time is normally shorter than a full day at nursery.

You will have to look at your work patterns so you can pick your children up after school. Your discipline may differ from that of the school, so you should consult the teachers.

As children grow older they may pick up bad habits by copying their friends at school, which can cause problems with your household routine. Also, as the children grow older, they have more after school activities that impact on your contact time, schedule and routine.

Teenagers

Changing a routine to one for a teenager will involve curfews, dating, ensuring the child takes on added responsibility around the house and does their homework. You should also factor in time for the computer and/or games console, homework and possibly a part-time job. The routine might also be affected by additional sporting activities and perhaps tutoring, and the fact they are allowed to spend time with their friends without adult supervision. All of this means change, including alterations to bedtime, and you must be prepared to be flexible.

The teenage years are tricky. Hormones are racing and your children are likely to test you by trying to buck the routine. They may rebel and try alcohol and drugs and you need to watch for the warning signs (see page 242). You can start to give teenagers more involvement in the routine and any changes that might be needed by giving them a copy to keep with them.

Breaking the rules

Children of all ages will always test your boundaries, so it is important that you let them know you will enforce the routine and so will their mother. If possible, have the same rule-breaking consequences at both homes, or children might try and play each off against the other parent.

The consequences of misdemeanours will vary depending on the age of the child, but could include:

- Time on a naughty step (see page 86).

- Earlier bedtime.

- Limit play time with toys.

- Reducing TV or computer time.

- Reducing pocket money.

- Reducing curfew.

- Added cleaning jobs around the house.

Children respond better if they are aware of the consequences of their actions and know what will happen if their actions are inappropriate. Put a chart on the fridge or notice board and discuss with your children what will occur if routine and rules are broken. You are likely to find that once they try it a couple of times and you follow through on punishment, it won't happen again.

The critical element here is not to be afraid to enforce the rule; they won't love you any less or want to return to mum's house. They will respect you, although you should be prepared for a few tears and tantrums.

The golden rule

After divorce, a couple become two separate entities. Each independently sets up a new home and many start doing things differently. Some redecorate their home in a different way to their old house; others take on new activities, jobs, even new friends. All of this is to mark the ending of one part of their life and the start of another.

When it comes to the children's routine, however, things should stay the same, as far as possible. Sometimes parents disagree about individual house rules, which culminates in a failure to agree over routine.

My golden rule is to stick to my routine and simply say, 'We don't do that at my house.' I never say. 'Your mother might let you do that, but not here,' as that is divisive. I simply reinforce the routine and rules I have at my home. Never denigrate your ex or her techniques. There is room to be flexible between households, but when a pattern of behaviour or a routine develops that adversely affects your household, discuss it with your ex.

TOP TIPS FOR WORKABLE ROUTINES

- Routine provides security for your children and is crucial post-divorce.
- Establish a routine the moment the children start spending time with you and include your ex-wife if at all possible, so that both houses have similar bedtimes and meal times.
- Ensure as best as possible that the routine is the same as prior to divorce or the same as the one they experience at their mother's house.
- Have a routine list that goes on a notice board and reward children for sticking to it.
- As children grow routines change, so ensure you take this into consideration and also inform your ex-wife.
- A parenting plan makes life easier for everyone. If you don't have one that includes a routine, consider using a mediator for the first year post-divorce if you and your wife don't get on.
- You and your ex should show a united front when disciplining a child for failing to follow routine. Ensure you follow through with punishments.
- As children get older discuss the routines with them and be flexible about new ones.
- Remember the golden rule: 'We don't do that at my house.' Never denigrate the children's mother.

Chapter 7

Communicating with Your Children

Being able to communicate effectively with your children is an important parenting tool. However, learning to talk to them and listen to your children during and after the divorce process is even more critical.

Divorce affects every member of the family in a different way. It is not just a husband and wife splitting up, but also a family unit breaking up and being redefined. Many times, it is the children who are hit the hardest. So, as a father you should understand that communication is crucial if children are to come through the divorce process, and it becomes even more important post-divorce.

Redefining communication

Prior to divorce, within the family unit you may have worked full-time and had a long commute home, while your wife may also have worked or cared for the children. That would have left limited time for communication and one-to-one time with your children. Many families do not even eat meals together. At the weekend, families scatter with various sports and other hobbies being pursued. If you have teens in your family, they are often self involved and if you get a grunt from them as a hello you are lucky!

When you and your wife decide to divorce you have to communicate this to the children: a tough conversation to have. Now, you have to start making more time for your children. (See page 13 for advice on how to tell your child about divorce.)

After the divorce, you have to redefine the way you communicate with your children when they are with you and that will take effort. You and your ex now live in different homes, but are bringing up the same children. As a great dad, you must develop a businesslike communication strategy with your ex to ensure you do not revert to childlike behaviour that could put your children at risk. It is tough, but you have to put your children first.

Learning to communicate at your house

It might be the case that prior to your divorce, you were not particularly involved in your children's life due to work commitments. But now you are responsible for them when they are in your home, so you must work at communicating effectively with each other. This means you must work out ways to break down barriers that may have developed during the divorce process. Develop a working relationship where you both talk to each other and make time to talk and be open and honest with each other, even about tough or embarrassing issues.

Whatever their age, this can be tough. With toddlers and youngsters, their language skills are limited so you will have to rapidly develop recognising non-verbal communications. Then there are the petulant teenagers who won't talk, so be prepared for a hard time. However, a good communication plan will help, and as your confidence grows you will develop good communication skills and a good relationship with your children.

First reread The Language of Your Post-divorce Life (see pages 21–29). Remind yourself of the importance of not using negative words about the experience you and your family have been through. Replace the negative with the positive. With older children, you can explain what you are doing. You could perhaps show your teenagers the list of negative divorce words and talk to them about how they felt. Then show them some positive alternatives or together come up with your own alternative positive words and phrases that you can use to refer to that bad time in everyone's life.

According to a study completed in the US by Arthur J. Schneider, a human development regional specialist, University of Missouri Extension in Cooper County:

- Dads who became more involved in parenting after the divorce had closer relationships with their children. When a father's relationship with his ex-wife was good, he spent more time with his children and assumed more responsibility for their upbringing.

- Children who have the opportunity to get to know their dads after the divorce may find they are not what their mothers portrayed.

- Fathers who have matured over time are able to improve their relationships with their children.

- The child's age at the time of the divorce makes a difference in how he or she experiences marital break-up during the early childhood years.

- Fathers who make it clear that they love their children and are interested in their lives develop better relationships and find learning to communicate with their children post-divorce much easier.

So, it is critical that you work as hard as you can to have positive communication with your children. Remember three key facts:

- The younger the child, the easier it is to develop positive post-divorce communication skills. You will be with a two or three-year-old as they learn to speak and if all they have ever known from you is love, attention and lots of talking and positive communication, that will follow through.

- With older children, especially teenagers, you will have to work hard at redefining how you communicate with each other, work through issues that might have developed and perhaps have counselling, because the way you communicated with children of this age during married life will change dramatically after divorce.

- You also have to consider your ex. If she is not adopting your businesslike approach, she might still be using negative language around the children and speaking negatively about you to the older ones.

How to improve communication

As soon as the children of whatever age know about the divorce, start setting aside time each day (if the family is still living under the same roof, or every time they visit) to talk to them as a group and individually about how they are feeling, how they are coping and what you can do.

Improved communication can start by just reading a book to them at night, doing some craft during the day or going to the park and chatting about what you see. Remember to do it every time you see your children. Once the divorce is announced, your window of opportunity to keep open the lines of communication starts closing and the children might start taking sides.

Remember the key rules: never speak negatively about their mother and ask the mother to do the same, and always speak positively about their new post-divorce life.

Conversations with your children

Children can shut down after divorce. The car ride from their mother's house to yours might feel uncomfortable during the adjustment phase, so here are some suggestions of questions you can ask to break the ice:

- What did you do at nursery/school today?
- Who is your favourite teacher?
- What is your favourite TV show?
- What is your favourite book?
- What would you like to do the next time you are at my house?
- How are your friends?

Older children enjoy discussing sport, music, computer games and out of school activities. With younger children, simply sitting and playing and talking about favourite toys helps to develop strong bonds.

Remember though that children at different ages have different developmental language and understanding. So the younger the child, the simpler and shorter the explanations and chats the better. The older the child, the more intellectual the conversation can be. Don't be afraid to do some research; if your child likes a certain band, Google it on the internet and impress them with your knowledge.

If your children have a question, it must be important to them, so take time and treat it with the care and consideration it deserves. Never just say, 'Ask your mother.' Children want answers and you have to provide them.

If it is a question that relates to their mother, never be sarcastic or mean spirited. Simply say, 'I'll check with mum and get back to you if she has an answer for us.' This is crucial because it means if she doesn't answer it is not just the child being let down, but you as well and the child does not feel as neglected. You will then have to be honest with your child and tell them, 'I have asked mum about the question you asked me and she didn't have anything to say about it. I am sorry. Perhaps you could ask her yourself or would you like me to try again?'

Let your children know from an early age that they can ask you anything without fear of consequence. Create an open atmosphere by being encouraging, supportive and positive.

Communicate your values

It is important to raise your children with a certain set of values and standards of behaviour. They need your moral guidance, so you should make your beliefs clear.

With older children, you and your ex should agree who will discuss the issues of sex and drugs with them. If it is you, make sure your ex knows when you have done it and vice versa. You should both be prepared for follow-up questions, which should be answered without embarrassment. Find out what they are being told at school and discuss it with them. See page 239 for more advice on this.

Listen

We all have busy lifestyles, but listening to your children while loading the dishwasher gives bad signals. For example, if you serve your child a meal and then go and start cleaning the kitchen, it is likely they won't eat it because they want your attention. They certainly won't talk to you, because you have given the impression you are too busy to chat.

Give your children specific one-to-one time and listen carefully. It builds their trust, confidence and self-esteem, and respect and trust in you. It also helps you to understand what the children really want to know and what they are ready to understand and learn about. It also keeps you from talking above your youngsters' heads and confusing them even further.

Phones off! I've lost count of the number of times I have seen a parent answer a mobile phone while their child is trying to tell them some big news. It is disrespectful and devalues your child's views and hence your relationship with them. Similarly, if your child sees you on your phone when they arrive back it deflates them and makes them feel like second class citizens. They need your full attention. Only answer the phone if it is an urgent call and explain that to your children.

Honesty

Children need honest answers and explanations no matter what age. If you don't provide a straightforward answer, your children will think either that you are lying or that you don't respect them. They will return to their mother with negative reports and confused views and that can cause problems between you and your ex.

Be honest. Tell your child you don't know the answer to a question, but say you will do some research and get back to them. Then hit the computer or phone and find the answer. If you don't give a truthful answer, children are likely to make up a fantasy explanation and that means their trust in dad is lessened.

If a child asks you about a negative event that has occurred during the divorce, you might not want or need to share all the details of a situation. But do not leave any big gaps, because children tend to fill in the blanks themselves, which can generate a good deal of confusion and concern.

Be patient

Young children often take ages to get their story out and you may want to finish sentences for them. Don't. It is their story and they take pride in telling you. Don't cut them off or tell them you will listen later. Be patient and be prepared for them to tell you the same story over and over.

Dads who allow their children to think at their own pace and tell their story will develop better communication skills and have children who know their parent is interested in their life.

Use everyday opportunities to talk

Doing regular things is a great time to talk. A great divorced dad truly appreciates the importance of taking regular time each day to talk to his children. It doesn't have to be highbrow; listening to jokes and stories is a normal part of growing up and is not exclusive to non-divorced families. Everyday talk is even more vital in divorced families, especially if you work full time. Your time will be limited, so give as much of it as you can to your child. For instance:

● Going shopping – talk about what should be on the shopping list.

● Walking to school, discuss with younger children the colours they can see, get them bird spotting or talking about their friends.

● Having a bath – talk about why it is important to be clean or what happened that day.

● With teens talk about homework, what they want for dinner, weekend plans and the things that interest them.

Repeat important concepts

Most children only take in small pieces of information at a time and will not learn all they need to know from one chat. So go over important issues again and again. This will also give you the opportunity to correct any misconceptions and to fill in missing facts.

Children often go away and come back and ask lots of questions: 'But why, dad?' is a constant one. Don't brush them off. Answer the question and ensure they understand that they can ask as many questions as they like because talking is good! Don't be afraid to initiate discussions repeatedly, either.

Patience and persistence will serve you and your child well.

Children communicating with mum when they are at your home

Any child has the right to talk to his or her mum or dad, irrespective of where they are. But you must set ground rules with your ex and the children about this. The time you spend with your children is special and it is your time, and should not be interrupted by their mother without a valid reason.

Sometimes care of the children becomes the subject of a, occasionally vicious, custody battle. Parents think custody is about winning or losing. It is not: it is about the children. Today more and more dads are being granted shared residency, but even if the mother has residency, it should not mean she has the right to dictate what happens at your home when the children are with you. No matter what arrangement you have, the mother does not have the right to call you, text you and 'pop around' when the children are with you on the pretext of checking everything is all right.

You have the right to say no, unless, of course, you agree or want the same right when the children are with her. But this is confusing for the children and can end in them witnessing arguments. The best option is to agree some of the following:

● Text or call if a major accident or illness occurs.

● If a child has been unwell at their mum's house and it is your day, get her to agree to text you an update on the child's health when at her home. The same should apply in return if the child is ill at your home.

● E-mail reminders about school or nursery events.

● Respect each other's privacy with the children.

Children under the age of four

Children under the age of four usually work easily into post-divorce routine and look forward to being at dad's house or mum's house. You should agree that you will only contact your ex when the children are at your house if there is an emergency, such as a serious illness or accident.

Children of this age will rarely ask to talk to their mother when they are at your house. Their focus will be totally on you. If they do ask to speak to their mum, run through a checklist first:

● Why do you want to talk to mum?

● Can I help?

● What's wrong?

Reasons why they may ask to talk to mum include:

● They are having a tantrum.

● They have not settled into your rules and want attention.

● Items they play with at mum's house might not be at yours and the children are trying to play their parents off against each other.

● Mum has told them to ask to talk to her as a control mechanism.

● They have not yet settled into the two-home routine.

● They may miss her in the same way they miss you when they are at her house.

Most importantly, remember that they probably ask to speak to you while they are at their mum's house, as well.

If your child really wants to talk to mum, make the call but explain to your ex that you are calling at the child's request and that you have given them permission. The last thing you want is the mother using it as a drama to come rushing around. It sets a bad example to the children and spoils them.

Children over the age of five

The same rules as above should apply. However, more and more children are being given mobile phones from an early age and you might need to monitor their use.

Ensure that you set a family rule that if they want to call mum from your house they check with you first. You might need to ask your wife not to text or call your children while they are with you. It interferes with their routine and can give the impression that mum and dad are getting back together.

But of course there are circumstances in which it is fine for them to call, text or e-mail their mum. Even then, limit the call time and ask your ex-wife to respect this:

- They want to share good news, such as a good exam result.

- They won a sports game.

- They want to know if a certain piece of clothing is there.

- They have other significant news or need her permission for an event they are participating in during her time, e.g. a sleepover.

You can also agree to allow a five-minute chat during the stay at your house at a prearranged time to show the children that their parents are working together. Again, this must be reciprocal so you can call your child when they are at their mother's, particularly if custody arrangements are week on-week off with each parent.

Remember: for both you and your ex, being separated from the children for nights and weekends is tough, especially if you do not have a new partner. When the children are there, it is great; but when they are with their mum it is natural to miss them and want to check up on them.

Their mother will probably feel the same. Appreciate and understand this, but learn to trust each other. If you both do your jobs well, it shows the children they can be happy and content at either home. If you do not trust each other, then this can become a flashpoint and further hurt the children.

Communicating with your ex-wife

As discussed on pages 43–45, a businesslike approach is often best. The key rule is never to ask your child to pass mum a message. If you can't talk face-to-face or on the phone, use e-mail, letter or text. If communication is difficult, hire a mediator for a period of time and meet once a fortnight or monthly. Have an agenda and discuss only children-related issues. As time goes by, your relationship will improve.

Dos and don'ts

If you do reach a point where you and your ex communicate effectively in some form like text, e-mail or phone there are some critical dos and don'ts:

Dos

- Encourage the dad's house/mum's house concept to help the children grow in positive ways.

- Communicate to your children that it is OK for them to love both parents.

- Treat each other with respect for the children's benefit.

- Respect each other's child-raising views by trying to be consistent. For example, if one parent strongly opposes toy guns for small children, the other should take this into account when buying gifts.

- If either parent takes the children out of town for the night, the other should be informed.

- If the children are left with other people, such as babysitters or friends, the other parent should be told.

- Try to agree on the children's religious education, as well as who is responsible for overseeing it.

- Parents should have each other's current address and home and work phone numbers.

- Accept that the number of nights the children are with each parent does not mean the person has a lesser responsibility for working at all levels of communication.

Don'ts

- Don't make your children feel guilty about spending time with their other parent. Communicate that fact regularly.

- Don't use seeing the other parent as a reward for good behaviour, and don't withhold access to the other parent as punishment for poor behaviour.

- Don't tell your children you will feel lonely and sad if they visit their other parent; this communicates guilt.

- Don't withhold seeing the other parent to punish your former spouse for problems such as missed child support payments. Withholding access punishes your children.

- Don't use false accusations to justify withholding access.

- Don't arrive late to drop-offs. Even if you are only five minutes late, out of respect you should text to say you are on your way to prevent your ex worrying.

- Don't let activities such as sports and hobbies interfere with the time your children spend with their other parent. Your ex can transport the children to those activities if needed and can sometimes participate.

- Don't pressure your children about leaving clothes or toys at their other parent's home. The children need to feel they belong in both places.

- Don't falsely claim that your children are sick to stop them going to the other parent.

- Don't withhold phone calls to your children from their other parent, but agree time limits and the number of calls. Revisit these rules regularly.

- Don't put down the other parent's new romantic partner.

- Never badmouth your ex to the children. If you want a positive relationship, you must set a positive example.

TOP TIPS FOR COMMUNICATING WITH YOUR CHILDREN

- Acknowledge that if you want to be a great divorced dad you must become completely involved in your child's life and reassess the way you communicate with them.

- Start early and set aside special one-to-one time for each child just to chat and hang out when they are at your house.

- Use everyday opportunities to start conversations like shopping for groceries or walking to school together.

- Research their favourite subjects and show an interest in what they do.

- Be honest and open with your children and answer all their questions. If you can't tell them the answer straight away, do some research and always get back to them.

- Communicate your values.

- Take time to listen to your children. Eating together is a great way for fun family conversations.

- Remember: younger children take longer to tell a story and love asking 'Why?' over and over.

- Always be honest with your children.

- Turn off your mobile when you are talking to your children and give them your full attention.

- Make sure they can ask you anything and tell you anything.

- Keep conversations about their mum positive.

CHAPTER 8

The Importance of Positive Discipline

Keeping up the discipline with your children after a divorce is critical to being a good father.

The difficulty is that your time with your children is very precious, particularly if they spend more time at their mum's house than at yours. So you might be tempted to allow them to misbehave, rather than spend that precious night dealing with discipline. You want the time to be fun and enjoyable for both you and the children. You might let discipline become lax because you think your children will:

- Love you more if you are more lenient than their mother.

- Want to spend more time with you if you are less strict.

- Want to spend even more time with their mother if you dole out discipline.

As a result, many fathers turn into what some experts call Disneyland Dads or Funtime Fathers. The children are not kept to their routines, not disciplined and try to take advantage of the situation. You have to stop doing this, as it:

- Sends a negative message to the children.

- Is bad for your relationship with your children, causing them to disrespect you.

- Will cause problems with you and your ex.

The role of routine

Many children misbehave because they either do not have a routine to guide them or you are not enforcing their routine.

Routine and discipline go hand in hand, and it is important that you as a dad establish a viable routine for your children at your new home right from the start. With babies, the routine will already be established, and you should be aware of that. To double-check, ask your ex-wife to write out the routine she has with the baby at her home, so you can keep to it. Do the same for older children, too. See pages 58–69 for more on routine.

Discipline plan

It is important to remember that your children need to view you as someone who loves them and yet someone who is also an authority figure whom they respect. They do not need a pal who lets them get away with things they are not allowed to do at mum's house. That attitude is corrupting and against the businesslike approach discussed earlier (see page 43).

You and the children's mother need to have a consistent discipline plan. Prior to divorce it is likely you had discipline strategies in place, such as time out zones, the naughty step (see page 86), curfews and extra chores for rule-breaking. Even so, in many marriages one parent is the disciplinarian. The arrangement is lost when you divorce and can result in neither of you disciplining the children because you are both trying to cope with divorce stress, money worries, new custody arrangements and a new lifestyle. If you are on good terms, review your discipline plan together and write down what you decide.

Discipline standards for both homes should be a part of your co-parenting plan, if you have one. Critical elements of a discipline plan are:

● What behaviour is acceptable and what is not.

● What type of discipline method is used for what sort of bad behaviour.

● The commitment that if a discipline starts at your house and the child returns to the mother's house that night the mother continues to carry it out, and vice versa.

● Commitment to co-operate on discipline to show mutual respect between the parents.

● Commitment by both parents to prevent your children using it to play you and your ex off against each other.

If you have a bad relationship with your ex, you will have to develop and carry out your own discipline strategies. Below are a series of discipline methods that work well and allow the child to understand limits, while at the same time enable you to carry them out and not be perceived as a monster. If, as part of the businesslike approach you are adopting, you feel it appropriate to tell your ex about your strategies and ask for her commitment to support your methods, do this in a clear letter.

Discipline for two to five-year-olds

Children in this age group present myriad discipline problems. You will have heard about the terrible twos, the flighty threes and the feral fours or fives. Remember that this happens to most parents and can be controlled.

At this age children may begin to misbehave for a range of reasons:

● Deliberately to test your limits or to see how much more freedom they can be allowed. For example, when playing with toys they may decide to start throwing them around the room first to get a reaction and then to see if this is allowable behaviour.

● They want more attention from you. They might be angry about someone else getting more attention.

● They are bored or frustrated.

● They are tired, hungry or over-stimulated.

How to stop this behaviour

Ensure your children have a safe environment to play in. Reward and praise good behaviour. At the first signs of trouble, try and distract them to an alternate activity.

When they misbehave get down to their level, look your child in the eye and firmly say, 'This is not a nice way to behave. I do not like this at my house. Please apologise and pick up your toy.'

Even at this young age, your toddler should be able to follow simple rules and if you consistently use the same firm voice, maintain the eye contact and reinforce your command you should be able to find the child will behave.

When you are disciplining a child they are getting the attention they want, even if it is negative attention, so try this reverse position. Do not get involved in power struggles with your children. Do not try a UN peace negotiation; it will not work, because at this developmental level a child cannot make multiple choices. Show a three-year-old five different outfits to wear and he is likely to get upset, confused and even cry; but give that same child two options and he will make a choice. So offer two options: behave and be praised or do not behave and be punished.

If your child refuses your commands and the bad behaviour continues and starts turning towards a tantrum, you will need a specific plan and a clear, consistent strategy. Your children must be aware that there is a consequence for bad behaviour. One such strategy is to use a naughty step, stair or chair to enforce a time out (see below). Use this with younger children rather than sending them to their room because their room contains fun things to play with and you lack the facility to check they are not hurting themselves.

The naughty step or time out zone

If a child starts having a tantrum or ignoring commands, go down to their level and tell them firmly to stop the behaviour.

If it continues, give one further warning and tell them they will have to go to the naughty step for a time out.

If the behaviour still continues, walk to the child, pick him up and sit him on the naughty step. Calmly tell them they are to remain there until they stop crying or misbehaving. Use a firm voice. Do not yell at them or use sarcasm. The time they stay on the naughty step should be one minute for every year of age, so for a three-year-old this would be three minutes.

If he runs back into the room or follows you, turn around, pick him up, take him back again and repeat the command. He will scream and cry, but simply tell him again that when he stops misbehaving he may rejoin you.

Then focus your attention on your other children or something else. Give the impression you are ignoring the child on the naughty step.

It may take a few struggles but you *will* win this and it will not harm the child. It is a strategy that works, but needs you to remain strong and not give in, no matter how it tugs at your heart strings.

When the child has calmed down, let him come back to you. Tell him again why the behaviour was wrong, ask for an apology and then allow him to play again.

Use this technique every time there is misbehaviour and you will find it very effective. You can use this technique when outside the house; if you are in a café and your children start misbehaving, remove them from the table and find a naughty spot outside the café. If they are in the park, take them away from the others or to the car.

Rewarding good behaviour

A reward bag is a positive discipline tool for good behaviour. Collect together a bag of special, inexpensive treats for your child. I suggest a visit to the local pound store where you can buy cheap, small farm animals, plastic dinosaurs, books, balloons and the like. Also include a card that says the child can have three books read to them that night or do three jigsaws with you. Use the bag carefully but make sure your child knows it exists and that it is used to reward good behaviour or good deeds only.

You need to plan ahead. For instance, if you know your child misbehaves at the supermarket, offer a reward next time you go by saying if he or she does not misbehave and cry but sits in the trolley properly you will offer a reward from the reward bag. This method works very well, but be warned: it is not about bribery. The child should not expect a reward every time they go to the supermarket and behave. Next time just give them positive reinforcement and praise or encourage them to participate in the shopping experience.

Another option is a chart with pictures, so your child can get stickers for doing a task around the house. The tasks are easily recognised from the pictures. The example below is for a little girl.

	Mon	Tues	Wed	Thurs	Fri	Sat/Sun

Every time the child does a task, she gets a sticker. The end result is if the tasks are done each week, the child is given her pocket money or something from the reward bag.

It is crucial that you do not encourage bad behaviour. If small children discover they can get your attention by behaving badly, they will make habit of it. Ensure your children are getting enough face-to-face time with you to discourage them from trying to use poor behaviour to get attention. If they start behaving badly, institute the naughty step.

Discipline for five to nine-year-olds

At this age, children understand more than toddlers do and you can communicate more effectively.

Once your children are at school it is essential that, as a great divorced dad, you speak to their teachers about the discipline methods they use, explain the methods you use and see if they are compatible. Continuity with school discipline will help your child experience more consistency in their life and that can only be positive. As you probably won't collect your child from school every day due to custody arrangements, remember to ask if there has been any misbehaviour during that week you should know about.

You can use some of the same methods for five–nine-year-olds as for toddlers. For instance, the naughty step and time out work effectively and should be continued. But the reward bag should be phased out. Remember, too, that your reasoning skills with the older child will improve.

Never yell or scream, and at all costs you must never hit your child. If you think you are likely to, you must immediately walk out of the room until you are calm and back in control.

House rules

Now you can introduce a list of house rules to your children. This simply outlines what behaviour is good and what is bad. They can also be used to encourage children to carry out tasks in return for pocket money or extra time doing their favourite hobby for completing them, countered with discipline if they do not.

By this age you need to be clear about:

- Bedtime – weekdays and weeknights.

- Amount of television watched.

- Number of DVDs watched and when.

- Computer/games console time.

- Time on the phone to friends.

- Pocket money.

- Homework.

By the time a child reaches the age of six you should consider drawing up a chart so everyone understands the rules and can measure whether they are being met. This dad/child contract, if you like, reminds everyone what is going on.

Below is an example chart for a young boy. Each day you and, in this case, Ben record whether he went to bed on time, list the time he watched TV – e.g. between 4pm and 5pm; same for phone use, DVDs watched, and so on. Ben knows his limits and can say to his dad, 'Look, I have done everything correct this week. May I have my pocket money, extra time on the computer or go skateboarding with my friends, please?'

Ben's daily rule record

	Monday	Tuesday	Wednesday	Thursday	Friday	Saturday
Bed by 8pm						
One hour of TV a day						
Two DVDs a week						
10 minutes on the phone a day						
30 minutes of computer time a day						

Removal of privileges

If a child does not behave you should start removing their luxury items. Identify with the child a list of items or activities he will not be able to use or do if he is naughty. You have to plan ahead because suddenly screaming at a child and saying, 'Right, that's it; no more ballet for you!' is confusing and they have no way of understanding what misbehaviour will prompt what punishment.

So be clear and write a list of what misbehaviour will result in what punishment. For example:

Misdemeanour	Punishment
Failure to do homework	No TV
Breaking curfew	Not allowed out with friends
Not cleaning room	Less computer time
Not helping with dinner	Reduced phone time
Not folding clothes	Loss of 10% of pocket money

Involving your ex

If the removal of liberties is to be successful, it is vital that you try to involve the children's mother. For example, if your son has misbehaved and you have said no TV for two days and on day one of the ban he is returning to his mother, you need to explain to her why you have disciplined him in such a way and ask that she continue the punishment. Most parents will be glad of the support.

Discipline and teenagers

Dealing with teenagers whose parents have divorced is often very difficult. However, you need to continue through with the strategies suggested above. Keep going with the charts, but add an actual written contract to the behaviour deal you have brokered with your teenager (see page 92). This is a grown-up document and the teenager can use it in conjunction with the chart and have a clear set of guidelines.

If you don't put things in a chart and written form, you give your teenager the chance to push the boundaries further. Here you have a reference point and a more logical way of reasoning with your child.

Removing privileges is the best method for dealing with negative behaviour in a teenager. Be clear with what the teenager will lose if rules are broken. It is also critical that you talk to your teenager's teachers. Their bad behaviour at home could be caused by something at school like bullying, influence of friends or problems with their studies.

Good behaviour contract

I Sarah Smith agree to:

- *Be in bed by 9pm on a weekday and 11pm at the weekend.*

- *Study for two hours a day.*

- *Complete all my homework on time.*

- *Watch only two hours of TV a day.*

- *Watch no more than five DVDs a week.*

- *Be on time for school.*

- *Call dad or mum if I am going to be late home.*

- *Participate in my basketball group.*

- *Assist with the housework.*

In return, if I complete these things to the satisfaction of my dad, John, I will receive £10 pocket money a week, £10 a month for my mobile phone top-up and the right to have friends over on the weekend I spend at my dad's.

If I break the rules, dad can choose to restrict my curfew, remove the television from my room, ground me and cut my pocket money.

Signed:

Sarah . . . .

Dad . . . .

Divorce and negative teen behaviour

Some negative teen behaviour may be the result of the divorce. Some teenagers take the split badly and:

- Blame themselves for your divorce.

- Dislike the new routine.

- Dislike the new partners of you or your ex-wife.

- Dislike the disruption to the life they knew as their family.

- Be upset about the sale of the family home and the purchase of two separate properties.

- Feel ostracised by friends.

- Feel it is a sign of being unloved.

- Feel they are asked to take sides.

If your teen is experiencing these feelings, negative behaviour will result and this might include acting up at school. Where possible, talk to your ex-partner openly about it and both try to sit down with the teen to discuss the issues.

Teenagers have the right to decide which parent they want to live with or may ask to be given a say in the custody/visitation arrangements. Listen to them and take on board what they say, because it might help them to settle and focus their attention back on their education.

However, remember routine is crucial, even for a teen, and getting to the bottom of the problem is critical. So, again, whether you like it or not, you and your former wife must work as a team on this one and not expect the other parent to bear the burden alone. You will have probably noticed this is one of my mantras when it comes to being a great divorced dad: trying to involve the mother in dealing with issues, and ensuring routine and continuity. For many former couples anger still pervades, but you *must* try to put this aside. Your children's needs must come first if they are going to live positive post-divorce lives, so for their sake you must make the effort and adopt a businesslike approach.

Teen angst

Teen angst is a normal part of life, whether you are divorced or not. But as a great divorced dad it is important that you keep a watch for the key indicators discussed above, ensure your child knows he or she is loved, has a routine at your home and knows that you are not afraid to step in and take action if things get bad.

It is possible that your ex-wife will blame you for your child's bad behaviour and won't agree to help you. She might even deny that the teenager behaves the same way at her house. This could be because there is an ongoing custody battle. There can still be a lot of anger, divorce addiction, concern over money issues, a desire to punish the ex-spouse for whatever caused the break-up, or conflict over who has the more power over the children and therefore in the relationship.

If your ex refuses to discuss the child's negative behaviour, admit it or if she blames you for it, consult friends or your lawyer, with the view to putting your child's interests above those of your own. Then:

● Talk to the school.

● Spend more positive time with them.

● Inform your ex via a businesslike letter or through your lawyer what you are doing and why, emphasising that you believe your actions are in the best interests of the teenager and that you are not placing blame at anyone's door.

Counselling, either as a group or individually, is a good option. By speaking to a third party your troubled teenager can independently reveal his or her true thoughts and hopefully work through the angst, feelings about the divorce or simply why there has been a sudden change in behaviour.

TOP TIPS FOR POSITIVE DISCIPLINE AND ROUTINE

- Don't be a Funtime Father. You have to discipline as well. Don't think your children will hate you because you discipline them.
- Positive discipline offers security.
- Provide a safe environment that encourages exploration but establishes boundaries.
- Don't assume that their mother is disciplining them.
- Be consistent in your methods of discipline and how you punish your child. Try and discuss co-ordinated discipline strategies that work at both houses.
- Set up a daily routine for your younger children and try to stick to it. This should include meal times, snacks, bath and bedtime, because failure to keep to routine will spark misbehaviour and tantrums in young children.
- Set limits that are appropriate for your child's age and developmental level. Some limited give and take is OK, especially with older children and adolescents. Listen to your children's input on some rules and punishment.
- Don't offer choices in situations where your child has to co-operate with your rules. For example, instead of saying, 'Do you want to take a bath?' you should say, 'It is time for your bath.'
- Don't give in to your child when he is whining, crying or having a temper tantrum. If you do, it will only teach him that this kind of behaviour is an appropriate way to get what he wants.
- Use the phrase, 'We don't behave like this at my house,' to be clear about what you expect.

- Don't negotiate. Be strict and clear with your children about the consequences of breaking the rules.
- Ignore any protests. You can talk about it later.
- Use the naughty step and time out.
- Keep visual records of things the children do that are correct and help them earn towards a reward.
- Use a reward bag. Make rewards immediate, but do not resort to bribery. Once good behaviour patterns are established, such as washing hands before a meal or helping with tidying, stop using the reward bag. Set the bar higher and give the child a new goal to aim for.
- Plan ahead. If you always have difficulty in certain situations, such as prior to handovers, shopping or having visitors, go over a plan of action beforehand.
- Use discipline and routine contracts, especially for older children.
- Use 'I' messages, instead of 'you' messages. For example, say 'I am upset that you didn't clean up your room,' instead of, 'You upset me by not cleaning up.' 'You' statements can seem more accusatory and can lead to arguing.
- After disciplining your child, briefly explain the rule and what your expectations are when he misbehaves and explain what the proper behaviour would have been.

CHAPTER 9

Children and Food at Your House

As a father of two children, one thing I know for certain is a family that eats together stays together. The children eat more of their meal, are less likely to be distracted, they chat more and feel safe and happy, and feel like part of a proper family unit – which, of course, they are.

Many mums and dads feed their children separately from themselves and while the children are eating mum and dad are doing other things in the kitchen like loading dishwashers, cleaning and talking on the phone. This is not good as it makes the child feel less important and more prone to not eating; if you start that cycle, convincing them to eat is tough. I always eat with my children and they clear their plates and enjoy the family chat.

This also means that you teach your children good eating habits and table manners, so you can happily entertain or take them out to restaurants, confident that they know how to behave.

Why eating right is crucial

Many dads find the concept of cooking for children quite challenging. You might not understand the importance of good nutrition or how to cook basic yet wholesome food that will help your children grow into healthy young people. This chapter will help you.

Your children are growing on a daily basis. Their bodies do not stop developing until around the age of 18 and for a body to develop correctly it must have the correct materials, i.e. food.

Children also need fuel to supply them with energy, and while chocolate may be a quick energy fix, it is not healthy for prolonged energy release during the day. As a parent, it is important that you care about what goes into your child's body as much as you do about their clothes, education and health.

Eating properly and eating quality food also means a child is less likely to fall ill. Their ability to fight off colds is stronger and less illness means a more positive outlook on life.

Finally, there is the question of maintaining a healthy weight. The UK, for instance, has the highest childhood obesity rate in Europe, and has become a nation of junk food giants. While the odd burger and chips as a treat is fine, on a daily basis it is just plain wrong; not to mention that it makes your children sluggish, unhealthy and more susceptible to serious diseases, such as diabetes.

So it is your job as a great divorced dad to learn to cook, to ensure your children are healthy eaters and to make this healthy eating positive and fun. This means that you have to eat properly, too, in order to stay healthy. Do not allow yourself to slip into bad eating habits. A Pot Noodle and a can of lager is not a meal!

Food pyramid

To understand the building blocks of good nutrition for you and your children, you need to have a basic working knowledge of the food nutrition pyramid (see page 99). This will help you understand what you need to ensure your child eats on a regular basis to have a balanced diet.

So what does the pyramid actually mean in real terms for you as a dad sitting across the table from your hungry child or teenager? The following is a summary of the basic food groups and what this means for your children:

- **Fatty and sugary foods:** includes biscuits, chocolates, soft drinks and confectionery. They provide empty calories and should be kept to a minimum. Avoid foods that contain saturated fats.

- **Essential fats and oils:** good fats, found in nuts, seeds, olive oil, sunflower oil and oily fish.

- **Dairy foods:** includes milk, cream, yoghurt, cheese, fromage frais, even custard and rice pudding made with custard. They are a rich source of calcium, essential for strong bones.

- **Protein:** includes lean meats of all types, fish, eggs, beans, nuts and soya. These foods are essential for growth and repair, and provide iron and zinc and vitamin B.

- **Fruit and vegetables:** provide vitamins and minerals, fibre and phytochemicals to boost the immune system.

- **Grains and potatoes:** includes multigrain bread, pasta, rice and cereal, which are rich in complex carbohydrates, fibre and minerals. Whole, unrefined grains are nutritionally superior to refined, such as white bread. These foods are the biggest part of your children's diet.

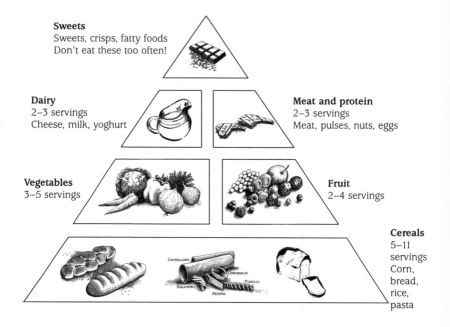

Sweets
Sweets, crisps, fatty foods
Don't eat these too often!

Dairy
2–3 servings
Cheese, milk, yoghurt

Meat and protein
2–3 servings
Meat, pulses, nuts, eggs

Vegetables
3–5 servings

Fruit
2–4 servings

Cereals
5–11 servings
Corn, bread, rice, pasta

What defines a portion?

That is a great question and, believe me, when I first started cooking for my children I was confused about the whole issue. So here is a simple rule: do not try to force your children to eat the exact amount of food portions from each nutritional group each day. Look at their intake over a week and if it evens out, you are doing a good job. You could use the eating plan table on page 101 to help you monitor your children's intake, but do not let it become an obsession.

Note: These portions are for two–six-year-olds. Increase them percentage-wise as the child gets older. Do not overload the plate as this can be intimidating. It is better to give them seconds rather than a huge plateful that will not be eaten.

Food group	One portion
Grains: six portions a day	1 slice of bread, 15–30 ml/1–2 tbsp cooked rice or pasta, 15–30 ml/1–2 tbsp porridge, 15–30 ml/1–2 tbsp pasta, half a potato, a small bread roll, and 15–30 ml/1–2 tbsp ready-to-eat cereal
Vegetables: three portions a day	Half a carrot, 1 floret of broccoli, 15 ml/1 tbsp peas or beans, 15 ml/1 tbsp spinach, 15–30 ml/1–2 tbsp other vegetables
Fruit: two portions a day	Half an apple, orange, pear or kiwi fruit, 1 plum, 2 strawberries, 1 apricot, 4–5 grapes
Dairy: two portions a day	1 cup of milk, 40 g/1½ oz cheese, 1 pot of yoghurt, fromage frais or homemade custard
Protein: two portions a day	1 slice of lean ham, chicken or turkey, 40 g/1½ oz lean minced meat, 1 organic sausage, 1 small egg, 15 ml/1 tbsp lentils or beans
Essential fats and oils: one portion a day	10 ml/2 tsp nuts or seeds, spreads using olive oil, olive oil used for cooking.

Eating plan: did we eat enough of the right foods?

	Sunday	Monday	Tuesday	Wednesday	Thursday	Friday	Saturday
Breakfast Milk Meat Vegetables Fruit Grains							
Snack Milk Meat Vegetables Fruit Grains							
Lunch Milk Meat Vegetables Fruit Grains							
Snack Milk Meat Vegetables Fruit Grains							
Dinner Milk Meat Vegetables Fruit Grains							

After every meal, you and your children can put a star next to the food group, one for every portion they have eaten. So, if they have two pieces of fruit as a morning snack, put two stars next to fruit and so on. It is a fun way of working out if you and the children are eating healthy. If you do really well, you can include a reward at the end of the chart.

Routine and monitoring food

It is also important to note how critical routine is in your children's eating patterns. Think how crabby you feel if you skip breakfast or how you feel by mid-morning and then tend to binge on junk food; or if you do not eat lunch how by dinner time you are experiencing low blood sugar and get angry more easily. It is the same with children. If they do not eat regularly, they will experience the same mood swings, tantrums and lack of concentration.

So set times for breakfast, snack time, lunch and dinner, especially with toddlers and children between the ages of five and twelve. No matter what you are doing or how important it is, stop and make the meal and ensure you stick closely to your routine otherwise you have confusion and a crabby child.

This means:

● You can plan your day.

● You will prevent tantrums and bad behaviour.

● The children feel secure and happy knowing when they will be eating.

● The children can look forward to eating breakfast and dinner with you (lunch will be at school) during the week and eating all meals with you during the weekend, when there will be a chance for you as a family group to chat together, adding extra post-divorce security.

You will also find that the need for discipline will be less and they will be happier and healthier.

When you are going out at the weekend, try to eat lunch roughly around the same time as during the week if at all possible. Always carry a healthy eating snack bag. I use organic crisps, carrot sticks, juice bottles, healthy sandwiches and fruit, so I always have something with me when I can see the signs that we have gone past the normal snack time or lunch time. These signs include:

● Irritability.

● Tantrums.

● Wanting attention.

● Whingeing.

● Bad behaviour.

● Answering back.

● Not doing as they are told.

Teaching good table manners

With routine comes your chance to teach your child correct table manners. It is a sad fact that millions of families do not ever have a meal together and just eat in front of the television. Do not allow this to happen to your family. Make dinner time special. Reward good manners and discipline a child for bad manners. Give the children your full attention and talk about your day or things that you are planning to do.

From as early an age as possible, encourage your children to sit properly, using the correct cutlery rather than their hands, and a paper towel, not a tea towel to wipe their sticky fingers. Yes, it will get messy, but the smile on their face when they cut their first sausage by themselves is fantastic. From the age of about three, insist your children put their knife and fork on their plate and say thank you when they finish their main meal, and please when asking for pudding. There is more about teaching children to feed themselves on page 210.

Insist the children ask to be excused from the table. I use the explanation, 'It is good manners. I do it and so should you.'

To get children started, offer little rewards for the child who eats the most, tries different or new types of food, displays the best manners and so on. If a child behaves badly, ignore him and pay attention to the child who is behaving correctly. If the misbehaving child realises that this is not the way to grab your attention, you are likely to have success. If that fails, use the naughty step (see page 86).

Toddlers and problem eating

Feeding toddlers can either be easy or tough. It is easy if you give in and go down the fast food path; it is tough if you decide to be a responsible parent and ensure your toddler gets the proper nutritional balance and learns to eat properly for later life.

Once you start preparing meals for your children, you might discover that toddlers:

- Can be picky eaters.

- Do not eat much, yet appear constantly full of energy.

- Throw tantrums until they get junk food.

- Suffer the 'sausage and chips only' syndrome, demanding the same food for every meal.

- Do not want to try anything new.

- Consider vegetables and fruit evil.

- Only eat one or two types of dinner.

- Eat for the nursery or babysitters but not for you.

I am here to tell you do not be alarmed. This is perfectly normal toddler behaviour.

Toddlers do not grow as fast as babies do. They may eat less than you expect, but if they eat smaller portions more often it helps keep energy levels up. They have smaller appetites and as long as they have energy and appear happy and healthy you are doing fine. You may then suddenly notice they want to eat everything on their plate. This is a sign they are on a growth spurt, so encourage that eating pattern.

Another way to encourage toddlers (and older children) to try different foods is to take them grocery shopping with you. Let them browse in the fruit and veg section and choose something they would like to try or that they think looks interesting. If you involve them in the purchase of food and let them help you make dinner, they are more likely to try new foods. My children and I grow our own vegetables, including potatoes, carrots and radishes. I discovered they would happily try the radish or eat all the potato if they knew they had grown it, harvested and cooked it.

But what about the food pyramid?

You are now probably starting to think about the food groups and how you can encourage your children to eat the right amount of the right foods every day. The best approach is to start slowly and to plan a three-day rotating menu that gives the child the basics and allows room for them to experiment with new foods. At each dinner I try to introduce a new fruit or vegetable and ask my child just to taste it. If they do not like it, fine; but they get praise for trying and it encourages them to start being adventurous.

However, the true key to making the food pyramid work is to learn how to prepare a basic range of meals for your children that provide a balanced diet. Be a good divorced dad and keep the ingredients you need for those meals in your kitchen cupboard. Then slowly experiment with new foods, gradually adding them to the menu and increasing the list of meals you can cook. It is also important if possible to involve the children in cooking the healthy meals and cook more than one meal at a time so you can freeze them, remembering to label the bag with 'John's Pie, Aged 4, Made 25 March'.

The more involved with food preparation your children are, the more they want to eat what they help buy and cook, the more likely they are to want to try new foods, and so the healthier their diet and the more positive and happy their attitude to food.

Your great divorced dad well-stocked kitchen

In your new house you will need a proper array of utensils if you are to be able to cook properly. This should include:

- Working kitchen – stove, oven and microwave.

- Toaster.

- Kettle.

- Set of non-stick saucepans and fry pans.

- Set of cooking knives.

- Fish slice.

- Wooden spoons.

- Egg whisks.

- Blender.

- Microwave cooking containers.

- Mixing bowls.

- Measuring jug.

- Chopping boards.

- Plastic storage containers in various sizes.

- Plastic plates, bowls and cutlery for small children.

- Cutlery set.

- Freezer storage bags or containers and freezer-proof pen.

- Biscuit baking tray and cake tins.

- Steps so children can reach work surface.

- Safety locks on cupboards storing chemicals or glass.

- Safety protector guard for front of stove for small children.

- Kitchen towel.

- Washing detergent.

- Hand wash – everyone should wash their hands before touching food, before every meal and snack. Make it part of your eating routine.

Now you have the equipment, here are the basics for your store cupboard:

- Baked beans or tinned pasta shapes – avoid cheap brands as they tend to have more sugar and salt than necessary.

- Rice.

- Dried spaghetti pasta and pasta shapes.

- Plain tomato pasta sauce and spaghetti bolognaise sauce.

- Tinned tuna.

- Tinned corn and other tinned vegetables as back-up only – fresh is best.

- Tinned tomato soup or vegetable soup.

- Vegetable stock cubes.

- Tomato sauce.

- Porridge – the sort that can be microwaved is quick.

- Child's favourite healthy cereal – avoid the sugary brands.

- Organic crisps (chips).

- Crackers, rice cakes.

- Soup croutons.

- Chocolate biscuits, such as bourbons, for treats.

- Chocolate stars as a pudding or treat.

- Bread – preferably brown or wholemeal or the white/wholemeal combined.

- Jam or favourite toast spread.

- UHT milk cartons as a back-up.

- Sugar.

- Salt and pepper.

- Hot chocolate drink powder.

- Sugar-free fruit squash.

- Fruit juice cartons – long-life.

- Flour – plain (all-purpose) and self-raising.

- Ready-mix cakes and biscuits – cooking easy packet mixes is fun and easy when you do it with the children.

In addition, you should keep the following in your freezer:

● Good quality sausages.

● Minced (ground) meat.

● Bacon.

● Organic chicken pieces.

● Healthy oven chips (fries).

● Frozen mixed vegetables.

● Frozen shepherd's pies.

● Frozen meat pies.

● Hotdogs – my children love the vegetarian variety.

● Good quality fish fingers.

● Bags or containers of extra portions of homemade meals – labelled and dated.

● Frozen pastry.

In the fridge, keep:

● Butter or sunflower spread.

● Milk.

● Fresh fruit juice.

● Organic yoghurts or fromage frais.

● Fresh vegetables – or keep these in a cool, dark place.

● Fresh fruit – but keep bananas at room temperature or they will turn black.

● Eggs.

● Fresh meat, fish or sausages.

● Ham.

● Cheese.

● Hummus.

● Special treats.

If your children develop a liking for a particular food, keep a stock in. My son loves chilli con carne, so I always have some in the freezer. I suggest you put a chalk board in the kitchen that you use to make up your grocery list, marking up when you run out of items and ensuring your cupboard is always full.

Shopping trips

Take the children with you to buy food and let them help select items from the shelves. Children have great memories, so get them to remind you what is needed. Encourage your children to add new foods to the list if there is something they want to try.

Doing one weekly shop works out cheaper than lots of short trips. Use a list and plan your menus beforehand to save money. Look for three-for-two or bulk deals on staple items.

Always check the labels on food to ensure the food does not contain too much sugar, salt and saturated fats. Most foods have labels listed by proportion. Try to buy organic when possible.

Suggested three-day menu

Now you have the staples and a plan for ensuring you update your cupboard regularly, you can devise a rolling menu to ensure that your children get all the items they need from the food pyramid over a three-day period.

Day 1

Breakfast: porridge with banana, toast fingers, juice.
Snack: fruit slices and crackers.
Lunch: baked potatoes with cheese and baked beans, yoghurt.
Snack: mini ham sandwich soldiers and cheese slices.
Dinner: spaghetti bolognese, rice pudding.
To drink: milk or organic juice. Always have water available in non-spill containers.

Day 2

Breakfast: shreddies or shredded wheat with warm milk, toast soldiers with jam (jelly), honey or cream cheese.
Snack: ham and cheese wrap, rice cake.
Lunch: bacon and chicken risotto, fromage frais.
Snack: cheese and fruit platter, sweet biscuit.
Dinner: organic sausages, carrot, broccoli, mashed potato, mini sweetcorn.

Day 3

Breakfast: organic bacon, canned pasta and toast soldiers.
Snack: healthy muffin and fruit.
Lunch: chicken or beef casserole with homemade chips (fries) or rice.
Snack: rice cakes, fruit and cheese.
Dinner: baked ham, sweetcorn, carrots, peas and gravy.

More ideas to make meal times go well

Breakfast

- Use pastry cutters to cut toast into different shapes.

- Cook different types of fruit and wheat germ into muffins.

- Offer different cereals and let children mix and match and discover what they like.

- Serve organic juice for breakfast.

- Try being innovative – try breakfast in bed or breakfast in the garden; or take your children out to a café occasionally.

- Cook porridge with creamy milk. To encourage children to eat, add their favourite fruit, such as chopped apple or chopped dried apricots.

Lunch and dinner

- Create pictures with the food for younger children, e.g. use vegetables to create a face or an animal shape.

- Blend additional vegetables into your pasta sauces.

- Offer rewards for the person who cleans their plate, shows the best manners or helps with the cooking.

- Take your children to restaurants from an early age.

Easy meal options

Once you get your confidence and your children start requesting your special wiggly worm pasta made from chopped spaghetti or other meals, start being adventurous:

- Good quality fish fingers, homemade chips, mushy peas and sweetcorn.

- Simple chicken stir fry with wiggly worms.

- Fish pie with mashed potato topping.

- Homemade burgers.

- Tuna pasta.

- Children's homemade pizza.

- Toddler curry.

- Spaghetti bolognese – vegetarian or meat option.

- Toddler risotto.

- Toddler casserole.

For lunch, try:

- Organic soup and crackers.

- Ham, cheese or chicken sandwiches cut into unusual shapes.

- Mini toasted sandwiches – use the biscuit cutters to make different shapes.

- Homemade chicken nuggets.

Snack options:

- Children's muffins – add bran and apple sauce to sweeten.

- Fruit platter – with a small dipping bowl of strawberry purée or melted chocolate.

- Fruit smoothie.

I have included some easy, children-friendly recipes on pages 211–217.

Children and vegetables

Let's face it: all parents want their children to eat more vegetables and fruit, but it can be tough. I have come up with some innovative ways to hide vegetables and fruit and so ensure that the children get their daily allowance.

Pasta method

This is the great way to get your children to eat vegetables. Make some basic tomato sauce, then cook a range of vegetables and blend them into the sauce very finely. Because the sauce is red the children will not notice the extra blended vegetables. Stay away from leafy vegetables, though, as the green bits tend to get noticed. What works well are carrots, corn, potato, peeled courgette and cauliflower. Add the sauce to the pasta and bingo! vegetables in their stomachs.

Casserole method

If your children are finicky eaters, use the pasta sauce above as a tomato base for casseroles. Alternatively cook the casserole as usual, then 20 minutes before serving stir some of the vegetable-enriched sauce into the gravy and cook through.

Soup method

All children have their favourite soup. Mine love tomato soup and they particularly love their 'chicken granny's' homemade tomato soup, which is full of chunky bits. If I have not had time to make soup, I use a can of organic tomato soup and add in some cooked and finely blended vegetables.

Pie method

Most children love shepherd's pie, mince pies, steak pies or chicken pies. If your children fall into this category, the vegetable tomato sauce can be added to homemade pies. It is perfect because the veg are disguised with pastry and sauce. If you use a white sauce with chicken pie, use less colourful vegetables, such as cauliflower or parsnips.

Quiche method

Replace some of the egg and milk mix with some cooked, blended vegetables.

Fruit smoothie

If your children love milkshakes or junk-food shakes, you can replace them with a healthier version by making a fruit smoothie. Blend together 1½ bananas, half a cup of apple juice, half a cup of orange juice and a handful of strawberries or blueberries to give a lovely rich taste. The banana creates a soft, silky, milk-like base. Children love experimenting with different combinations of fruit.

Divorced dad's secret fruit sauce mix

Peel and slice five eating apples and put in a pan with 100 g/4 oz prunes and about a cup of orange or apple juice. Add a little water if necessary to cover the fruit. Bring to the boil slowly and cook until the fruit is soft. Blend until silky smooth; the mixture should be the texture of very thick jam. Use this mixture as an alternative to fat or dairy products, replacing up to ¾ of the amount, e.g. in muffins and cakes.

What you should and should not worry about

Many parents, particularly dads, are concerned about what is normal when it comes to children eating. Everyone has an opinion and after divorce you do not have your wife to consult with. So I have compiled a list of some common concerns and what you should do about them.

Don't worry if:

- Your children are not eating a lot. As long as they are active and healthy and putting on weight, things are fine. If you are concerned talk to the health worker or the doctor.

- Your child only eats one kind of food. It is not uncommon for children to demand only sausages or beans on toast. It is a phase and they will get over it. Do not actively encourage it and always offer other options at meal times.

- Your child will not try any new foods. Children are naturally wary. Also, they focus on routine, so if your child's nursery has a routine rotation of food, you could ask them to introduce new foods to expand your child's horizons. Introduce new foods slowly and offer a reward for trying them. I got my daughter and son to eat broccoli by calling them little trees, and corn and carrots by telling them they could bounce like a bunny if they ate them. Tempt them to try fruits by offering a treat from your reward bag.

- Your child does not eat a balanced diet each day. Let's face reality: most children *don't* eat a balanced diet each day. So as a dad, take a view of their diet over one or two weeks. The key is variety. Use the chart on page 101 to keep a record, so you can work out over a week where the imbalance might lie.

- Your child does not finish everything on the plate. It is an old-fashioned view that children should eat everything. Offer smaller portions and ask if they are still hungry. If you are worried, try limited snacks between meals. Children have small stomachs and small appetites. Encourage them to recognise when they are full and to tell you.

- Your child does not eat what you prepared. The key to toddler eating is keep things simple. Elaborate meals should be avoided. Children may not want to eat adult meals, but they can be tempted to taste. If they show an interest, let them experiment. I try to offer a taste of a new type of food every few days. Some toddlers like foods on their plate separate, so do not try mixing peas and sweetcorn; two separate piles is a much better idea.

- Your child is a picky eater. Is your child putting on weight and active? If so, everything is all right. But if you are worried, talk to the health visitor. Check, too, with the teachers to find out what they are eating for their school lunch.

- Your child will not eat vegetables. Try the methods on pages 112–113 for hiding vegetables and fruit. Involve your children in cutting the vegetables for dinner, let them help to cook them and decide their placement on their dinner plates, perhaps making faces or animal shapes.

- Your child gets constantly distracted while eating. This is a common complaint and I can tell you that normally an adult is to blame. If you eat your meals separately from your children, or are busy tidying the kitchen while they have their meal, they are bound to become distracted. It also makes the children feel less valued. So the key is eating together or, if you cannot do that, at least sit at the table and chat with them while they eat. Give them your full attention. Ensure the television is off and remove all toys or books from the table. The focus should be on the food and a dinner time routine. Remember that and you will decrease distraction and increase eating.

You should only worry if your child is not putting on weight, is lethargic or not very active or has a restricted diet consisting mainly of milk and juice. If your child is losing weight or simply will not eat anything, see a doctor and discuss your concerns and talk to the child's mother.

Also be aware that the UK has the highest child obesity rate in Europe. It is your responsibility to ensure that your child eats healthy, balanced meals and exercises regularly.

Teenagers and diet

As with younger children, the most important thing to remember if you want your teenagers to eat the right food is to lead by example. Ensure your children see you eating the right foods and encourage them to try bites of new and different foods and reward them for doing so. As children get older, try to take them out to different restaurants and perhaps let them bring a friend along. Let them try Japanese, Chinese, Thai, Korean, French and Italian. Encourage them to embrace food and enjoy it.

Teenagers also like cooking for themselves and I personally would encourage them to tell you what meals they would like you to cook for them – and get them cooking, too.

It is important to learn what foods your older children and teenagers like and to try and develop healthy eating options when it comes to junk food. There are always healthy alternatives for junk food favourites, such as oven chips instead of deep fried. Try substituting homemade grilled burgers and grilled kebabs with vegetables.

Children and cooking

Children love cooking. In some towns and cities parents actually book their three-year-olds into toddler baking classes, which simply entails the toddler rolling a piece of dough around for half an hour but it is still a class for which the parent pays handsomely. At nurseries they do the same as part of the day's routine. You can, of course, try the cheaper option by encouraging your children to join in the kitchen fun from the moment they can sit up.

Most parents declare the kitchen a no-go zone, but not me. I allowed my children to sit safely on the kitchen bench, supervised at all times, and let them mix things, crack eggs and be involved.

I have discovered that if children are involved in the food preparation, then they are more likely to eat their meal. They are more relaxed about foods and more likely to try the taste of new fruit, vegetables or meat than if they are banned from the kitchen. Having said that, it is important to remember that the kitchen is a dangerous place, so make sure that wherever your child has access it is safe and all sharp knives and other implements are removed.

As your children get older, put their names on the rota for washing-up, setting the table or cleaning the kitchen.

Eating out

I believe it is important for you to take your children out to cafés and restaurants from as young an age as possible and to do it regularly. They learn a great deal by example and you will find their social skills develop as quickly as their palate. This may also be helpful for dads who only see their children away from home due to custody arrangements because they live in a different town or country.

It is a great family activity plus it gives your children a chance to try new foods. As they get older, encourage them to bring along their friends, if you can afford it. Many parents think taking children to a restaurant is a nightmare and a chore. It is only that way because you as a parent view it that way or put up with your child's ratty behaviour. But if you teach them it is fun and reward good behaviour, they should behave.

I started taking my children to cafés from the day they left hospital. By two years old they could sit happily playing in their buggy for 20–30 minutes in a café while I had a coffee. By two-and-a-half, I had developed a café strategy and kit that I still use.

- Recce beforehand. Check the venue is child friendly. Make sure the menu includes child dishes or that main courses can be adapted to suit children. What is the order time of the venue you choose? If it is renowned for being slow to bring food to the table, do not take your children as they will get bored and hungry after about 15 minutes. This is the maximum time you should allow for between ordering and the food arriving. After that, children will start running riot.

- Ask for a 'baby chino' for small children. This is just an espresso cup with only the froth from the top of a cappuccino (naturally no coffee or hot milk, in case it spills) and chocolate sprinkles on top. The children get a spoon and think they are very grown up. For older children, allow them to try hot chocolate with marshmallows.

- If you are out for lunch or dinner and you have two toddlers with you, order one child-size meal and two plates and split the food between them. This cuts down on money and waste.

● Restaurants that offer tapas-style taster dishes are great with children as they can experiment.

● For young children bring a bag of fun things with you – I always have some stickers, crayons, paper and a couple of books or a puzzle with me in case one of the children gets bored too early.

● Make it a weekly or fortnightly treat and as the children get older they get to choose the location. Allow older children to bring their friends along, too.

● Tag going to a café to another event, like a sporting activity, or do it after a swimming lesson or other similar activity. This ensures they are hungry, they have done some physical exercise and they will enjoy the café more.

Junk food dilemma

It is a dilemma that every parent faces: how to stop or limit your children's access to junk food. For divorced dads it can be even harder, because the children may beg to be taken to McDonald's or Burger King as a special treat when they are with you and you want to keep them happy.

I have a set of rules regarding junk food:

● Avoid introducing your children to fizzy, sugar-filled drinks for as long as possible. I do not have them in the house.

● Limit access to sweets.

● Make a trip to the chip shop or McDonald's a special event that occurs rarely.

● Ensure your children's school has a healthy eating policy.

● Talk to your children about the damage junk food can do.

● Develop homemade alternatives to junk food – it can be fun!

Top tips for healthy, happy meal times

- A hungry child is a crabby child; a well-fed child who eats around proper meal time routines is a happy, contented child.
- A junk food-eating divorced dad is grumpy and negative; a healthy eating divorced dad is positive and full of energy. Lead by example.
- If you can, get everybody to eat the same meal together. Avoid cooking separately for yourself and your children. It means you all eat together, saves time and the children follow your example.
- Know the basics of good nutrition, but do not become obsessive.
- Learn to cook, and encourage your children to become involved in all aspects of food preparation, from shopping to washing up afterwards.
- Instil good table manners.
- Don't worry about problem eaters. Most problems are normal behaviour and resolve themselves in time.

Chapter 10

Entertainment and Outings

A fter divorce you might find that your ex-wife has more time with the children. It may just be an extra night, but it does mean she sees the children more than you so it is only natural for you to feel the time you have the children is extra-special and that every minute must count. The next two chapters will show you how to do that. But the key to be being a great divorced dad in this area is:

● Routine.

● Planning.

● Not being a 'Disneyland Dad' or a 'Funtime Father'.

● Not being afraid to discipline your child because you think they will love you less or not want to spend time with you.

Routine

As we have already discussed, children of divorce particularly need routine in all elements of their life. It gives them security, especially when they are spending time at two different homes and coming to terms with new family structures. Routine is also important when it comes to entertainment and outings. It is important that you differentiate between normal routine outings, which are done on a daily or weekend basis when the children are with you and thus allow you to structure and pre-plan your day, and non-routine outings, which are special events and treated as such.

The most important fact a divorced dad must realise is that you don't have to do super-exciting outings every time the children are with you. Feeding the ducks or going to the park is just as important as a trip to the circus or the pantomime (see below). Don't make the mistake that many divorced dads initially do by treating their children to theme parks, weekends away and other expensive outings every time they are with them. It spoils the child and sets a precedent.

So, what is a routine outing and what is not? Take a look at the table below. You will see that routine outings can be done weekly or perhaps every second weekend, if you are one of those dads who has a custody arrangement in which you see your children every second weekend. Non-routine outings may take more planning.

Routine outings	Non-routine outings
Feeding the ducks	Trip to the beach
Going for a walk	Trip to a children's fun park
Kite flying	Visit to a farm
Going to the park	Visit to an aquarium
Going to the cinema	Visit to a zoo
Going to a café or out for lunch	Birthday parties
Bike riding together	Visit to specialist child fun centre
Grocery shopping	Tenpin bowling
Horse-riding lesson	Clothes purchases
Visiting grandparents	Visit theme parks
Going to church	Pantomime visit
Visiting a family with other children	Big family gatherings
Swimming lesson	Firework nights
Ballet lesson	Town festival and parades

When you create a table like this, get your children's input. Ask them what they consider routine outings and entertainment, and what they consider to be special treats. That way they can create a wish list of things they would like to do with you either regularly or on special occasions. Involving them in planning makes them feel special and builds confidence.

Remember that as part of instilling discipline at your house (see page 83), it is important that children earn their special outings and entertainment, and understand that these outings cost more. Everyone has to save for them or they perhaps have to do extra chores around the house as their way of contributing to the special event.

Planning

Now that you have your list of routine and non-routine outings, you need to consider the importance of planning. My top tip is that forward planning makes for a better time for you and your children and it gives everyone a sense of security. I always plan ahead when it comes to time with my children because:

● It helps me maximise the quality time I spend with them.

● I can pre-book any special events.

● I know what events are occurring, I can allow for their effect on meal times and if necessary prepare food to take with us.

● I can talk to the children in advance to see if what I have planned suits them or is what they want to do.

● It allows me to involve other families, if the outing is suitable.

Planning when the children are with you

In the first post-divorce year, I feel it is important to keep a spreadsheet plan of the time spent with your children. There are two reasons for this: first, you will benefit from the assurance of routine; and second, should you have to go to court to resolve any issues over custody you will have a diary record of how the children spend time with their father, which might prove crucial. If possible take lots of pictures of your different activities as a record of what you do, showing that the children enjoy their time with you.

Below is a sample spreadsheet. Yours does not necessarily have to be this detailed. You can simply write in a normal diary in point form.

Friday 1 October	Activity	Comments
3.30 pm	Collect from school.	Got newsletter and a spare for their mother.
3.30–4.30 pm	Free play at home, did jigsaws, Lego and soft toys.	Separated mum's children clothes from mine and washed uniforms.
5–6 pm	Dinner prep and dinner as a family – sausages, potatoes, peas and baby sweetcorn and pudding	All ate their dinner, helped with clearing up.
6–6.30 pm	DVD of children's choice	*Finding Nemo*
6.30–7 pm	Bath time and reading	Loved new book *Squash and Squeeze*.
7.30 pm	Bedtime	Both went OK
Saturday 2 October		
7.45 am	All up, toilet, toothbrush hand wash and dress.	Got stickers on chart for tooth brushing.
8.15–9 am	Help with breakfast – bacon, sausages and beans	All ate together and discussed day.
9.30–10.30 am	Swimming lesson and after-lesson snack.	
10.30–11.45 am	Grocery shopping.	Everyone helped at Asda getting things off shelves and reward was a magazine each. My daughter got to choose a new pink skirt and my son a spider t-shirt.
Noon	Home for lunch – spag bol and pudding.	All ate well.
1–2 pm	Quiet time and nap.	Children allowed to play in bedroom, Tom slept for 30 minutes.
2–3.30 pm	Granny visit and she and I took children out on their bikes to the park.	

4–5 pm	Free play	Tom requested trains and Julie Barbies. If they want another toy, they must tidy up others beforehand.
5–6 pm	Dinner prep and dinner – chicken risotto and pudding.	
6–7 pm	Bath time and reading (no DVD tonight)	*Squash and Squeeze* and *Room on Broom*.
7–7.30 pm	Bedtime	Little resistance but promise if both go to bed on time they may watch an extra DVD on Sunday. It worked.

Another reason to forward plan outings

Forward planning for when the children are with you also means you do not have to waste valuable child time doing things like paying bills or getting the car repaired when they are with you. Here is a list of things you should get done when they are *not* with you:

- Essential bill paying and banking.

- Health care appointments for yourself, including alternative health care.

- Visits to places that are likely to involve queuing, e.g. renewing your car tax.

- Car repair and maintenance.

- Major house renovations, unless you are doing it and your children are teenagers and want to help.

- Dating – prior to introduction of new person to your children.

- Clothes buying for you.

- House cleaning – if necessary hire a cleaner once a week for a couple of hours the day after the children go back to their mum's, to help you keep the place tidy and neat.

- Major clothes washing and drying – although at the age of four my children love helping to load the washing machine, sort clothes and put their clothes away. so consider letting them help.

● Food shopping – although, as above, I like taking my children food shopping and did so from the moment they were born. They love going to the supermarket and helping get things off shelves and they also love picking out their own clothes. If they behave they get a reward, and it teaches them that this is part of everyday life.

● Menu planning for when the children are with you – important because it means you have a stocked fridge and can control spending.

● Plan what routine and non-routine outings you will do on your time and if necessary book lessons or tickets to avoid disappointment.

Keep a diary to plan when to do these mundane but essential tasks and ensure it is all scheduled around your child's schedule.

Don't forget when making your plans that your children might also have their own regular commitments. These might include music lessons, sporting commitments such as football practice or gym club, Brownies, youth club and so on.

Café and restaurant outings

I find it incredible that more dads, and mums for that matter, don't take their children to cafés and restaurants. I have discovered that some cafés get asked by schools if they can bring in classes of children to teach them how to order toast and hot chocolate and to teach café manners. Taking your children to a café as an outing can be fun and if you work it into your routine for lunch or a snack you can avoid fast food venues and at the same time teach your children manners and show them how to behave around other people.

There is more about taking children to cafés and restaurants in the previous chapter (see page 117).

Recommended outings bag

I always carry a bag containing the following:

- Stickers.
- Paper.
- Crayons.
- Colouring book.
- Small puzzle or favourite toy.
- Magazine for older children, especially puzzle magazines.
- Story book.
- Bag of organic crisps, couple of biscuits in a ziplock bag, small carton of juice, tin of ready-to-eat pasta shapes or a tin of soup, just in case menu does not cater for your needs.
- Sealed bag of old bread for duck feeding – you never know when you'll spot a lake of ducks.
- Small first aid kit – you can buy kits that fit into hand bags.
- Wet wipes.
- Spare knickers for younger children.

Ideas for non-routine outings

These outings are special occasions to reward good behaviour, as a celebration, to recognise an achievement or to mark a special event. If the visit is to be designed around good behaviour or children sticking to their routine, let them know; if they have a goal they are more likely to work positively to it.

From the age of about four upwards, you should ask your children for their input into what they want to do for these special outings. What they think as something special might not be something you have thought of. It could be something as simple as a visit to an aquarium, farm, fun park or zoo, or perhaps a visit to London or other big town for a shopping spree for special toys, books or seasonal clothes. Consider the following:

- Concert (all ages).

- Theatre visit or a pantomime at Christmas.

- Cinema.

- Town parade or special town event.

- School fête or concert.

- Attendance at special classes.

- Face painting.

- Birthday parties.

- Special family gatherings.

Once you have decided what the special outing is to be, make sure that your children know why they are being treated to the outing. Set behaviour rules before you go and make it clear how you expect your child to behave

If it is a visit to a theme park or animal farm, perhaps you could invite some friends along – the more the merrier. Take a camera and record the event so you can relive it with your children and the friends they invite.

Ensure everyone eats on time and watch for signs of tiredness and grumpiness. Perhaps on special non-routine outings you may like to drop the no junk food rule and allow them to choose from the menu themselves.

If the outing is to the circus, concert or some form of theme park, give each child some money so they can choose what rides to spend it on. Ensure you remain as a group if your family is young. You might agree that teenagers can wander by themselves, but agree a time and place to meet.

Do not give in to whingeing. On some non-routine outings, a child may want every item in sight or to go on every ride there is. Stick to your guns. Don't ruin a fun day out with tears and tantrums on the way home.

Sport and action

Don't forget that sport can be a fun and healthy way to bond with your children. I strongly recommend getting out and involved with your children from an early age, not just walking them to the park and watching them play, but actually joining in with them. It makes them feel special and it can be an important part of routine outings and entertainment.

For two to four-year-olds

Try the following:

● Kite flying.

● Hikes – look at your local maps and find easy routes.

● Soft room play.

● General rough and tumble.

● Introduction to swimming.

Contact your local swimming pool for details about lessons. Some private gyms have pools that offer lessons, too. Take them swimming yourself, but ensure you follow all the water safety rules. Children under four might need swim nappies, arm bands or other buoyancy aids, as well as towels and swimming togs. Check with your pool, but the rule is generally that children under two need one-to-one care in the water. Even competent child swimmers need to be accompanied by an adult.

Five to ten-year-olds

As above, but also:

● Bike rides.

● Horse riding.

● Dance classes – these and other organised classes require the commitment of both parents.

● Sailing, boating or surfing, if you live by the sea.

● Tennis, cricket and soccer and other team sports.

Teenagers

Try some of the activities suggested for the under tens, but also consider:

● Gym.

● Skateboarding.

● Rock climbing.

● Extreme sports.

Now you can take part, organise lessons, cheer from the sidelines but make sure you are involved to the maximum degree. This is your chance to bond with your children and you must make the most of it.

Other sporting options

● Check with your children's school about after school sports sessions.

● Use Yellow Pages and the local paper to look for various father and child sessions – or pick an activity you fancy and suggest it to them.

● Use the internet with your child and find out what they would like to do with you, then find out how you can make it happen within your budget.

● Children's yoga – yoga centres, beauty therapists and some children's clothing stores might also have information on baby massage.

TOP TIPS FOR ENTERTAINING YOUR CHILDREN

- Distinguish between regular routine outings and special outings and entertainment.
- Goal-orientate the special outings.
- Simple outings are often the best; too much of a good thing spoils a child.
- Ask for your children's input on the type of outings you do; you might be surprised by what they choose.
- If outings are linked to classes, ensure you have their mother's approval.
- Always prepare in advance what you will do with your children on your days and get your work and chores done on the days the children are with their mother.
- Consider involving other families or your relatives if they live nearby.
- Always take an outing bag with you; it has been a lifesaver for me.
- Enjoy yourselves and have some fun – that's the aim of the game!

CHAPTER 11

Handicrafts and Rainy-day Activities

Previous chapters have discussed the importance of routine and focus in helping your children adapt to their new life after your divorce. The need for post-divorce bonding cannot be overstressed and one way to make it successful and fun without spending lots of money is by involving your children in craft and rainy-day activities. It may sound simple, but children of all ages love craft activities, making things from nothing, and if you are there to help so much the better. Taking the time to create a craft box will give you the opportunity to:

● Give your children your close and undivided attention.

● Strengthen the post-divorce bond.

● Have fun without spending a fortune.

● Make gifts for friends and family.

● Encourage creativity in your child.

● Make your child feel more secure and happy because you are getting messy and dirty with them painting, gluing and creating things.

It may seem funny, but after my divorce sitting around a kitchen table with my children making things from cardboard boxes, toilet rolls and paints was fun and positive. They seemed secure and happy and knew everything was well with the world. I would recommend that any divorced dad makes the time to do this with their children – it is great therapy for you and fun for the children.

Craft can be done any time, of course, no matter what the weather, but it is a fantastic option for a rainy day. When the children are stuck inside, you won't want them watching DVDs all day, so ring round some of their friends and invite a couple around and have a rainy day craft afternoon. It can be great fun and your children get to show their friends how cool their dad is when it comes to making things.

Half an hour of craft time helping your children make something will mean so much more to them than a visit to the cinema. Why? Because their dad is doing something with them, talking to them and helping them. Yes, you might find you are bad at craft to start with, but it will be a learning curve for both you and the children. So just enjoy it, and as you do your craft sessions talk to your children about school or nursery or what they have been doing. Remember: it is not what they make in the end, it is the fact they have made it with you.

But to get started you must have a well-planned craft box and a range of ideas and things to make and do with your children.

Craft box

You will probably have some of the basic craft box items around the house. What you do not have can be bought fairly easily from many high street shops or via the internet. See pages 248–249 for suggested suppliers. I also search eBay for children's craft items. I found you can buy great little kits for making foam photo frames. Even better, involve the children in selecting what they want to buy by having them sit on your lap when you are bidding! Remember to check the age specification on the kit you buy.

- Box or basket for items.

- Newspaper or plastic cover to protect the table and floor.

- Water-based paints and brushes.

- Containers for mixing paints.

- Plastic painting bibs for you and younger children.

- Children's scissors – left-handed, if necessary.

- Child-friendly glue.

- Sticky tape.

- Crayons, felt-tip pens – but beware of highlighters or permanent markers because they stain and the fumes can be quite strong.

- Roll of cheap lining paper from a DIY store or a ream of paper for painting and drawing.

- Coloured cardboard.

- Selection of material scraps (old clothes will do).

- Ball of string.

- Collection of different-sized polystyrene balls.

- Stickers.

- Feathers.

- Glitter tubes.

- Selection of stick-on animal eyes.

- Baby wipes for cleaning up.

You should also start a collection of empty kitchen roll tubes, egg cartons, small boxes, plastic bottle tops, pieces of foam or any other item you think could be used for craft.

Craft for children under ten

Children under five will need a lot of help. Also, their attention span is quite short, so be prepared to do as many as three different craft items in a 15–20-minute session. Once children reach four or five, their dexterity will have greatly improved. In addition, they will have started school, where the curriculum includes lots of craft activity. At this age, you can encourage more creativity.

Ensure that your children know what their craft space is. In other words, limit the area to a table and chair or outside on the lawn and no further. Otherwise trouble will ensure when they daub paint on the walls! If the child breaks the rule be sure to discipline and explain why.

Painting

From experience, I strongly recommend that you use a plastic sheet on the table and ensure that you and the children wear plastic bibs. A bath can remove most paint, but returning a child with paint on clothes can set you back months with your ex. Imagine how you would react if she were to bring the children to you in paint-stained clothes.

Young children will start with finger painting. Ensure that the clothes underneath are old ones, because no matter how much protection you provide, they will make a mess. Give them a couple of colours and show them how to start and let them go for it. Handprints are the best to start with and take it from there, perhaps experimenting with angles to create a tree or an octopus. The colours are likely to get all mixed up and end up brown, but who cares: this is super fun for the children and they are doing it with you.

They will probably finish a painting in about one minute and you must look at it and hang it up to dry using pegs and a piece of strong string tied across the room. After each painting is finished, children love to be praised and to have their work displayed and admired.

As the children get older introduce more foam shapes and brushes and suggest a theme, such as shapes or animals.

If you're feeling confident, cut up some card and bend it down the middle so that the children can paint cards for their friends or family members for Christmas or birthdays. Let them take them home to show their mum, not to show off what you have done but simply so you can say, 'Why not make a card for mum? It is her birthday' or 'Because you are getting good at this.' Also, painting large pieces of paper is a great way for you and the children to make wrapping paper for gifts.

Stamping

Child-friendly stamp kits are great fun and widely available. Just make sure that the stamp ink is not indelible. I would suggest farmyard animals and Christmas shapes, then you can make stamp cards, stamp pictures and other fun things.

Potatoes, coins, egg cups and potato mashers can all be covered in paint and used to make prints. Try painting on a plastic bag and then pressing that on to paper. Beware though: the stamps have a habit of ending up on walls!

If you use rolls of white paper, the children can stamp their own wrapping paper for that personal touch and use stamps to decorate gift cards. You can also make themed stamped posters.

Paper cutting

Children under four love ripping and cutting paper – using child-friendly scissors, of course. Children under two often get more fun out of wrapping paper than actual presents!

For a fun craft session, collect a bundle of magazines and some scissors and with your children cut out pictures and shapes, and glue them into a montage. When the children are old enough, come up with themes. For example, you could suggest finding all green pictures or red or blue things.

Hanging decorations for Christmas and parties

This is great fun but needs a little forward planning.

Before you start, cut some cardboard into various shapes such as stars, circles, triangles or squares, and punch a hole in the top. Cut up lengths of string and, if you are making a mobile, find a wire coat-hanger. You will also need glue, glitter glue, sparkles, small bits of coloured paper and chopped up scraps of fabric.

Give the children the shapes and let them paint them, or glue the fabric, coloured paper and glitter on to the cardboard shapes.

If making decorations for a Christmas tree, simply tie string through the hole and hang on the tree. If making a mobile, tie different lengths of string to the decorations and then to the wire coat-hanger and hang it up.

Cardboard craft

Let your children paint cardboard kitchen-roll tubes in different colours and then cut them up into about 2–3 cm/1 in lengths. Then string them together to make decorations or a chunky necklace.

Make buildings using boxes and cardboard tubes. Using a range of sizes paint the boxes or cover them with fabric, pieces of paper or whatever the children choose. Use a cardboard tube for the chimney.

To make a 'My Special Box', select a smallish cardboard box for each child and have them decorate the inside with fabric and the outside with whatever they choose from the craft box. They can keep special things they find in it, such as money, shells, pebbles or small toys.

Use your imagination. I made a chicken with the children using a kitchen-roll tube and pipe-cleaners for legs. Then we simply stuck on some coloured feathers and drew on eyes.

Nature craft

This is fun to do during the autumn. Take a bucket out and have the children collect autumn leaves, maybe some sticks and dried flowers. Bring them home and then use what you have found to make a montage on paper.

If you go to the beach, a great way to remember the adventure is to collect sand, pebbles and shells and layer them in a plastic jar with a lid.

Collect sticks of different shapes and then using glue, stick them on paper to make people and animal shapes. You can do the same thing with straws and washed ice-cream sticks.

Children love learning how things grow, so save some old yoghurt pots and plant quick-growing seeds such as mustard and cress, sunflowers or beans. The children can paint the pots and plant their seeds, and watch their nature craft grow. See also garden craft (page 138).

For the more adventurous, make a Mr Grassy-head. The children will need your help with this one. Put some grass or cress seeds in the toe of an old pair of tights or a pop sock, fill it with four or five big handfuls or soil and tie the end to make a round ball. Put the ball into a pot and then paint a face on it or stick on eyes and a nose and mouth. Water the top of the head regularly. As the seeds sprout, Mr Grassy-head's hair will grow.

Card-making

If your children have had to move town following the divorce, this is a great way for them to keep in touch with relatives or old friends, as well as for personalised cards for birthdays and other special occasions. Cards made by your children will have more meaning that ones bought from a shop.

Use a selection of coloured card cut into pieces 20 cm × 25 cm/ 8 in × 10 in. Fold them in half and then let the children glue on bits and pieces from your craft collection or colour their own pictures. You can also make a collection of cards on a theme, such as Christmas. You can help by making stars, drawing Santa or buying some Christmas stamps. Ensure you have envelopes and involve the children in the process of writing inside the card and on the envelope, putting on a stamp and taking it to the post office.

Masks

Many craft stores sell plain, full-face or half-face, white plastic or paper masks that your children can decorate with paper, paint, feathers – whatever you have collected. Alternatively, use thick card and cut out an oval with holes for eyes, nose and mouth. Make a hole at each edge and thread through some elastic then decorate the mask.

I have discovered this is a great thing to do with other friends when they come for a rainy-day play date.

Threading craft

Threading is a great, fun way to help your child develop fine motor skills. You can buy threading kits that comprise big buttons or cotton reels on to string or shoelaces. You can also buy bead kits, but check the age recommendation because beads can be a choking hazard. Alternatively, you can make your own kits by buying beads, buttons and thread from a haberdashery.

You can make necklaces and decorations for Christmas and birthday parties. This craft activity can be repeated over and over again, building your child's skill by asking them to thread only certain coloured beads or buttons or to thread in a pattern. Young children should never be allowed to play with string necklaces, as they can be dangerous.

Sand craft

Sand kits are widely available from toy shops as well as specialist craft suppliers. They contain a range of coloured, numbered sand bags and cards bearing pictures, often of favourite children's characters. The picture is made up of numbered stickers. Peel off the sticker and apply the matching numbered sand to create a picture.

I usually put the card on a plate to try and collect leftover sand. However, the children love mixing up the colours to see what it creates.

I often use the finished pictures as gift cards for the children to say thank you to their friends when they get invited over for play dates.

Garden craft

Children love gardening. It is the mixture of mud and water, and just the wonder of green plants and colourful flowers. So buy some compost mixture, some plastic flowerpots and some fast-growing seeds – radishes, sunflowers and beans are great – or some flower seedlings. Let the children paint the pots themselves before planting. If you have space outside you could give older children a small patch of ground to tend.

Plant the seeds and flowers and, all being well, over a few weeks the results will be great and the children can have pride in their growing works of art. Make it your children's responsibility to do the watering and weeding when they are with you. Keep a photo record of the plants' growth and create a 'My Plant Diary', so the children can show their friends and relatives and see the changes in each visit to you.

Also, try sprouting potatoes. They grow well in a bucket of soil and magically produce potatoes that you can cook and eat.

Sticker fun

Stickers are great. All department stores, book stores and toy stores sell vast arrays at very reasonable prices. I always have about five packets at home and my children and I do sticker art by drawing a picture and adding, say, flower stickers, Bambi stickers or whatever is favourite.

Always carry stickers when you go out, because if your child gets bored in a restaurant, perhaps, they can do some stickering – and gain you an extra ten minutes to eat or chat with a friend.

Stickers make nice thank-you gifts if you are invited over for a play date. They are also great for reward charts.

Kite making

If you search on the internet using Google, it will bring up several options of instructions on how to make a kite, but it is quite tricky to make one that flies successfully. (You could also buy a kite, but ensure your child picks it out.)

Flying a kite is a great bonding session and one that can continue through to teenage years.

Craft ideas for older children

● Threading craft – use smaller beads and make jewellery.

● Painting-by-numbers pictures and kits for painting their own cups and saucers or money-box. They can also start sketching and trying other mediums.

● Garden craft – older children can look after their own mini vegetable patch.

● Properly themed montages that can be cut up into jigsaw shapes to create jigsaws for you to put together.

● Sewing – start off with sewing cards and children's tapestry kits, then move on to simple napkins or basic dolls' clothes.

● Beading – a big trend and you can pick up kits for children from five to teenage years from toy shops.

● Toy-making – fairy doll kits (and others) are available. They need adult supervision, but the children end up with a toy they have made themselves.

● Papier-mâché – start with strips of newspaper glued on to a balloon, built up in layers. When dry, paint the balloon and decorate with a face or other design.

● Nature walks – walks can be longer and your children will develop their own sense of what they want to collect. Encourage themes and create a special area for their collections.

● Workshops – the school holidays often see schools and childminding centres run craft schools, art schools and sewing schools. If your child wants to sign up, try and go to some of the lessons yourself and learn alongside your child.

Teenagers

Once the children hit their teenage years, you will need to change the concept of quality time with you. By now your children will have worked out what craft they like doing: perhaps they are taking classes in art, video or photography. If you are skilled in these areas, teach your child yourself or learn together. Other ideas include:

- Redecorating their bedroom – they can do this with you. The project can include painting walls, making lamp shades (you can buy kits) and other items.

- Scrapbooks – encourage teenagers to put together scrapbooks of their time with you or create a family scrapbook and include everything from photos to ticket stubs, anything you find on your travels. Keep updating it; perhaps you could make a time once a month to add things to the book.

- Digital photography – work together on photographing a family album.

- Create a family website.

- Cooking meals – helping your children to cook meals may not be strictly craft, but it is fun and you can both experiment with different recipes for meals, cakes and snacks to make the most of it (see page 116).

Other options for a rainy day

- Cake making – I use the kits sold at supermarkets and you can start using them with children from three-and-a-half years under adult supervision.

- Make your own home video with the children. Pick a theme, e.g. each child gets to video their own room and talk while they do it.

- Get a selection of board games – even in the 21st Century they can be fun!

- Put on your waterproof coats, hats and wellingtons and go puddle-jumping.

TOP TIPS FOR RAINY-DAY FUN

- Prepare a craft box and a have a list of craft creations you can make from what is in your kit.

- Purchase some pre-prepared craft kits. They will help to build your confidence if you are new to craft.

- Be patient. You might have an idea of what the finished piece should look like, but children have other ideas; whatever it ends up looking like, praise it and put it on display. This makes them proud and builds their confidence. My children swell with pride when their artwork is hung up.

- Do craft as often as your can. Fit it into the routine at your house, so the children can look forward to it.

- Try out as many craft options as possible. Children get bored easily, so offer them plenty of choice.

- Try and work as a team to make Christmas cards for friends and relatives. You save money and they get a truly personalised gift.

- Encourage your teenagers to take craft to a higher level, perhaps website design or classes that you can do with them.

- Use the time to talk to the children and strengthen your bond with them.

- Remember: craft is fun and no matter how much mess it makes, the quality time you spend with your children is what counts.

CHAPTER 12

Education and Your Children

As a married couple, you will have jointly made decisions about your children's education, from nursery through to university. Some parents put their children's names down for certain schools the day they are born, while other parents may actually move to ensure their child gets into the school of their choice. However, the majority of parents choose nurseries and schools in their local area, with both parents discussing whether they are happy with the educational standards of the schools and, if relevant, whether they can afford it.

Early on, when the child is going to nursery or school, it is traditionally the mother who is responsible for organising the nursery and drop-off and pick-up. However, divorce changes that and it is important that, as a great divorced dad, you put education firmly on your agenda, no matter how old your child is.

Key to this is devising an education plan and agreeing it with your ex. Accept that the responsibility for your children's education, including financial implications, must be addressed and shared.

So if you are going to get involved, this might mean altering your work schedule so that you are there at the school gates to pick up your children on time. Employers are obliged by law to consider any reasonable requests for flexible working hours for parents. Or it might mean going to nursery coffee mornings dominated by mums, or baking cakes for the school bake if it happens to be on a day when the children are with you. Not only will this bring you closer to your children, but it will also put you more in touch with the carers, teachers and the education process as a whole.

Custody arrangements

If the court and CAFCAS decide residency and care arrangements, you and your ex-wife will be asked to make decisions about nursery or school arrangements, so they can be put into the court orders. This is a positive thing, because it gives both parents a say, it sets guidelines and it may allow many handovers and collection of children to occur at school or nursery. No matter how many people tell you they have an amicable divorce, seeing each other in the early stages can be tough. Children pick up on the tension, so handovers on neutral ground such as nursery or school can be helpful.

Note, too, that should you have to return to court to discuss custody arrangements, it can stand you in good stead in court if you can show that you have a strategic educational plan for your children. It is also worth noting that you have a say in the educational requirements of your children, even if you are the non-resident parent.

Preparing an education strategy

If you are not decided on nurseries and schools here are a few tips to help you prepare your educational strategy for your child.

Research local nurseries and visit them, talk to carers and parents and ask for references. Be thoroughly involved in selecting the place where your child will spend time. Find out the cost of nursery care and factor that in to your financial arrangements.

Choosing the right school is important so visit local schools in your area; ensure you live in their catchment area if this system is in place. Some smaller towns do not have catchment areas so that makes it a first come-first served basis. There may be other selection criteria, too. Even if you make an informed choice, you might not be awarded a place, so be prepared to battle or comprise.

Talk to the teachers, parents and get literature for your file about the school, including, in Britain, OFSTED reports. If you want to compare with private schools, do the same; but remember that what might have been affordable to you as a couple might not be possible after divorce.

Stages of education

The education system varies from country to country, but the following is the situation in England at the time of writing.

- Nursery – not compulsory, but some schools have nursery units attached to them that take children from as young as three. There are also external nursery units. It addition, some children attend some form of child care nursery from as young as three months if both parents have to work.

- Reception class – this is the start of formal education. In England, parents are required by law to make sure their children begin education from the beginning of the school term after they turn five. There are regional differences, but generally children will join a reception class at the start of the school year during which they will turn five, i.e. the September term after their fourth birthday.

- Primary education is from Year One to Year Six – up to 11 years of age.

- Secondary education is from 11–18.

- Instead of completing secondary education at school, children may leave at 16 to complete their education at college. Alternatively, they may leave at 16 to start work, perhaps with an apprenticeship.

- Beyond 18 is university or other higher education, sometimes preceded by a gap year.

Preschool child care

Your involvement with children's education begins even before they start school. If they attend a nursery, ensure both you and your ex see the application forms and that you have signed off on them. Make sure you have met the owner and staff and that the nursery has all your contact details in case of emergency.

Get to know the carers, talk to them about your child's progress and behaviour, and ask them for advice on things you can do at home with them. Nursery carers are a great source of information. For example, if you are having trouble with potty training, ask for their help; or if you want some advice on meals that the children like, ask for a copy of the nursery lunch menu and replicate that at home.

I found myself working closely with one of my nursery carers to create a special potty training chart that they could use at nursery to fast-track potty training. They were thrilled with my involvement and by working with them I helped my children.

When you collect your children try and meet the other parents, organise play dates and ensure you get a copy of the nursery newsletter (most do them now). Do not be shy because you are a man. You might feel shy, but if your work allows get involved in parent coffee mornings, or fêtes or other events. I altered my work schedule so I could do this, because I wanted my children to know their dad was interested in their education.

Always ask the staff how the children were that day. Then on the way home encourage your children to talk about their day. If they bring home drawings or crafts, display them on a special display board.

School: getting started

Prior to starting school teachers may visit your children at their home. You need to liaise with your ex-wife to find out at which house this occurs. If you have a good relationship with her and she lets you into her new home, be there for the visit.

If you have a bad relationship, make separate appointments to see the teacher. Explain you are divorced and could the teachers keep a second copy of the weekly school newsletter and other information for you, as there is never any guarantee your ex will give you a copy. Stress that you are concerned not to miss important events and dates.

Most schools also have an introduction session where parents bring their children and show them around the school, letting them see their classroom prior to starting. Again get involved in this. Perhaps your ex does the home visit and you do the school visit. For the children's well-being, try to put divorce anger aside when it comes to what is a huge change in your children's life.

Be involved in buying school uniforms. When I took my

children to buy their first school uniform they were really excited and wanted to wear it home. It meant a lot to them that their dad was interested and a great deal to me to be involved in such a big milestone.

On the first day, a positive post-divorce image is mum and dad both accompanying the child to school. No matter how much anger there is, this is an important day, so try as hard as possible to be there. If this proves impossible perhaps you could drop off the child and their mum collects, or vice versa.

Your child's reaction to school

Some children, especially those who have been to nursery make the change over to 'big school' very well. These children tend to be more socialised and cope easily with mum or dad dropping them off and leaving them. However, it is still a big deal.

At nursery before they start school they are the big children; now at school they are the babies again and at school there are older children all around them. Also, it is a new environment that they might only have visited once, with new teachers and different children. So talk up the event and encourage them to be brave and to 'help others'.

However, your child might be clingy, scared, whiny, or throw a complete tantrum and refuse to leave you.

Dealing with clingy and scared children

Children take their lead from their parents, so be positive about 'big school' and always discuss it as though it is a big adventure. Let your children pick out their own school bags, water bottles and lunch boxes.

Some parents feel guilty about leaving their child and a child will pick up on this and start crying or become clingy. So you must be confident and happy and explain what is going on. If the school allows it, walk them in and find their coat and backpack racks, show them the toilets, take them to the teacher. Quite often the morning session starts with the children doing a little free play, so find something your child likes and leave them to it. Ensure they know who is collecting them at home time.

If tears or tantrums start, follow the teacher's lead. Normally they will take the child and you should leave immediately. Within ten minutes they will be happily playing. For the first couple of days be prepared to take time to settle your children. Some parents arrive a little early and start reading a book to their child and then halfway through the book the teaching assistant takes over, thus distracting the child. The important thing is not to give the child an easy out and take them home again or ask for special treatment. This sends the wrong message.

If this behaviour continues, talk to the teacher. Perhaps your child needs to bring a special toy to school for a little while for security. Perhaps their mum has a different routine for drop-off. Always check with the teachers as they are the experts.

'Big school is scary' is a common complaint from younger children. So talk to your child to find out why. It could be a simple attention-seeking exercise, just like a child who suddenly develops a pain in the tummy as they walk through the school gates. If the problem continues, you should consider talking to the school counsellor either by yourself or with your ex-wife. It is important that you both work hard at finding solutions.

It is sad to say that in some divorce cases parents blame each other for a child's inability to settle at school and use this to gain greater custody. That is why involving teachers and possibly school counsellors is critical. They can provide a balanced approach that focuses directly on the child.

Older children starting new schools

Post-divorce families might have to move towns or the children may move to different schools because the new downsized homes are out of catchment areas. You must not forget that older children will be affected by this and it is important that you are there to be supportive.

Visit the new school with them and meet the teachers. See if the same team sports and after-school activities are available and get them signed up.

They are likely to miss their old friends, so try and ease them through this process by inviting their friends to stay or organising weekend get-togethers.

Be prepared for anger as teenagers blame this major disruption to their life, loss of friends and a new school on you and your ex. Talk to them and perhaps talk to the school counsellor about how to deal with the issue.

Being involved at school

Make sure you have copies of newsletters and other notices from school. Put up a wall calendar and mark on it school holidays, teacher training days when the children have time off, special functions, concert nights, parent-teacher evenings, fêtes and other events. That way you don't forget. I put mine in the kitchen and use a black marker to add things as they come along. It also means that with complex rotas for contact and extracurricular activities you can see instantly if events fall on days when you have the children.

Try to ensure you attend all parent–teacher evenings. Show your children you are a committed dad by lending a hand when parents are needed for school tidy-up days or sports days.

Make sure you collect the menu for your child's lunch if they don't take a packed lunch from the school's reception and check they have all the correct kit and talk regularly to the teachers.

It is critical that even if you and your ex are still angry with each other you call a truce for school concerts and sports days, and that on your weekends you take your children to sports events like soccer and stay to watch and cheer. These events are not baby-sitting alternatives; they are precious time with your children.

Great divorced dads always ensure their children's school uniforms and bags have iron-on name tags attached. You can buy these online. Also, regularly check the lost property bin – most classrooms have them. You should also regularly check your children's school shoes. Their feet grow quickly so you may need to replace them more than once a term. Teach the children to polish their own shoes; it is never too early to learn.

When you collect your children from school try and develop a routine. Walk if at all feasible. It is a great chance to talk about their day and the exercise will do you all good. Asking the children what they did, who their favourite friend is and so on is critically important. If you get the chance, ask your children to show you their work displayed around the classroom. Admiring it builds confidence.

Once at home, have a healthy snack prepared, such as fruit and crackers. Younger children who have just started school normally require a meal as soon as they get home. Otherwise they will eat too many snacks and spoil their appetite. Their bodies are growing, their day has been exciting and they will be hungry so this is a great chance to get them to eat a full dinner. I try and cook dinner and have it ready to go when they get home, so by 5pm we have eaten and can have some play time before the bedtime routine.

Get to know the parents of the other children in your children's classes and organise play dates and get-togethers. The children will develop a social life and you will find yourself developing one, too. You will also find your children will get invited to lots of birthday parties. If you receive an invitation that is not on your weekend, make sure your ex-wife sees the invitation. Ask her to reciprocate. Do not let your children miss out because you and your wife are still in the post-divorce anger period.

Homework

Even nursery and reception class children will have homework. Nothing taxing, perhaps a book to take home and read, but you have to make a note in their school book about their reactions. Make this part of your evening routine.

Ensure you know what homework is required. Younger children might be asked to bring in family photos, bake cakes or make craft items for special projects. Often classes have special dressing-up days or days they can bring a favourite toy. Don't forget these, because it embarrasses the child and means they won't feel like joining in.

Older children, particularly teenagers, have a great deal more homework, so talk to them about it and ensure you know what their teachers expect. Show you care by making a homework contract with your children. Set aside a certain time period after school when they have to do their homework, then when you have checked it they can do something they like.

It is important that you involve yourself in the homework process. This might mean simply checking that it has been done, and reading through essays and giving positive reinforcement. Or it might mean assisting your child if they are having problems – but be careful not to do the work for them. Avoid the competitive parent syndrome: parents have been known to do entire craft projects while the child simply watches! The key is you should assist, not do.

Another reason to know what your children are studying is that if you don't know anything about it you can do a bit of research yourself and be able to assist your children when they have problems. This shows you care. You could also offer to help your children revise at exam time.

If you feel your child is struggling, discuss with their mother and teacher whether a tutor is needed. If this should be the case, ensure the tutor is affordable, good at their job and able to work between two homes without being drawn into taking sides.

Term-time routine

Older children require routine while you also learn to trust them. So discuss when they do their homework, when they can have friends over, what time they have to be in bed and on weekends make sure you set time for:

- Exercise – ensure your older children get enough exercise and encourage walking or biking to school and joining school sports teams or doing sports activities with you at home.

- Homework.

- Music/sport practice.

- Fun time with you.

- Fun time with their friends.

It is important that similar routines are in place at both homes. A child that spends time with one parent that does not have routine and discipline, and then with the parent where routine is important is confused.

As already discussed (see page 83), discipline is crucial. No matter how you do it, try to discuss with your former wife or partner a routine that works the same way at both homes. If on handover a teen is being punished by mum for something, it is vital that you continue the punishment at your home. For example, if your ex has grounded the teen for four days and two of those days are with you, ensure you follow through on her decision and she should do the same for you. Do not send mixed messages to your teen by trying to buy their affection by ignoring discipline rules.

Both parents should have the same rules for:

- Computer usage – most teenagers use computers for homework so consider parental locks and content filters if they are connected to the internet.

- Time spent playing on a games console.

- TV/DVD watching.

- Pocket money.

- Curfews for parties and other activities.

Educational problems with older children

Teenagers claim they are misunderstood, parents shake their heads in dismay and teachers often do not know how to handle them. Sometimes it seems that youngsters reach a certain age and just kick off, misbehaving, testing boundaries, sleeping all day and bunking off school.

As a great divorced dad it is up to you to look out for the warning signs that your teen is misbehaving, because it means their education is being affected. The signs include:

- Falling grades.

- Not speaking and communicating with you.

- Hiding out in their rooms.

- Sudden change of dress style.

- Depression.

- Secretive behaviour.

- Missing curfews.

- Bad language and threatening behaviour.

- Running away.

If you notice any of these signs, start with the teachers and get their input by asking about your child's grades, whether they have been falling or remained static, and ask if your teen has been misbehaving in class.

Then talk to your child and involve their mother, if you can. Do so in an open, no blame way and you might find this works. However, if not that is where school counsellors come in. It is your job to care for your child's welfare, so set a timeframe for this phase that your teen appears to be going through. Try four weeks and then if the teenager's behaviour continues, take action and work with their mother on a solution that works in both houses.

After-school and weekend educational activities

Children from the age of four can have weekend or after-school activities. It might be tutoring, team sport practice, swimming lessons, ballet, horse-riding, tennis lessons, piano lessons: a whole range of things. It is important that one parent alone does not make the decision about these activities, because they are part of the child's education. Both parents must be involved and so must the child, who must want to do the activity or at least agree to try it out for a few sessions to see if they like it.

Agreement must be reached on which parent pays for the activity and kit involved.

You should also protect your agreed time with your child. If it is a weekly event at the weekend, it means your contact time is cut. Make sure you are all right with this or that the event is flexible, so that if you want to go away for a weekend with your children this does not conflict with the new activity. If you feel your time with your child is being reduced, negotiate additional time with your ex if it was her idea and if she has more time with the children. Flexibility is the key.

The activity must benefit the child, not the parent, and it is not an alternative for child minding or in some cases control mechanism on a former spouse. In other words one partner may organise tennis lessons each weekend for two hours thus controlling what the father and child do on their weekend at a certain time making you unhappy and the child feeling torn between parents or an activity and one parent's feeling about it. Do not be a showbiz parent; it is your child's life, not yours. Constantly reassess. Ask your child regularly if they are enjoying it. Some children will do things just to keep mum and dad happy and to stop them arguing.

Ultimately it is your child's decision if they want to do the activity, not yours. If they say 'Dad, I don't want to do it,' find out why, tell their mother and offer alternative activities.

University

By the time your children reach their A-levels you will have spent time talking to them about their future plans. Discuss them regularly and if possible talk to their mum about them. Encourage work experience during long holidays so your children can see what different jobs and careers are like. Whether your child wants to be a rubbish collector or a doctor does not matter; what counts is what makes the child, now a young adult, happy.

If they are planning a gap year, you need to start talking about this early. Talk to your ex and recommend a savings account into which payments are made if certain routines are stuck to. Additionally, the teenager can pay into the account if they have a part-time job, but not have access without your permission or until it is time for their gap year.

The same should be said for university. If you want your child to have a university education, start saving early. Take the lead and visit various universities on open days to help in the decision-making process.

Who pays for schooling?

Your lawyers will discuss financial settlements during your divorce and as part of this the issue of who pays for education will be looked at. However, you must both be aware that if you were fortunate enough to have had plans for a public school education prior to the divorce, this might no longer be affordable. This is because with parents splitting and each needing new homes, one parent may have to pay maintenance, the family may have to move to different towns and costs will vary.

If it becomes a sticking point, both parents might agree to pay into an education fund that will aim to cover public school costs· or even the costs of state schooling: things like school dinners, uniforms and shoes add up fast. If an agreement is reached put it into writing who pays what and when, and have it signed by you both.

It is also important to use this opportunity to agree which parent should pay for what when it comes to uniforms, sports gear, after-school events and so on, and how that will be arranged. While you probably think this is the last thing on your mind, if you dump an invoice on your ex for £250 for school uniforms or she simply expects you always to buy and pay for school items when a full and final settlement has been reached, in months and years to come you are likely to find yourselves back with your solicitors or in court.

Despite the divorce you should settle as early as possible:

- What type of education you want for your children.

- The nursery or child-minder to be used, if required.

- The school they should attend and how it will be funded.

- Who pays for what in terms of uniforms and after-school events, how the payments for school dinners and trips should be shared.

- Possible funding for a gap year and university.

A fund could be set up that both parties pay into or some form of investment purchased that can grow in value to fund post-school education. I suggest that when custody and financial arrangements are made during the divorce process you ask your solicitors to oversee the setting up of some form of university fund that you both pay into.

Putting it all down on paper and signing gives both parents clarity and focus so they can each spend less time worrying about the next fight and more time focusing on the children.

TOP TIPS FOR EDUCATION

- A great divorced dad is totally involved with their child's nursery or school, knows their children's carers and teachers and attends concerts, sports days and graduations.
- Think long term not short term. If you want your child to attend certain schools, plan early and be in agreement with your ex.
- Agree an education strategy in the custody and financial arrangements.
- Get to know teachers, other parents and your children's friends. Set up play dates, accept children's birthday party invitations and expand your friendship base. As a dad, don't be frightened to take the lead and go over to another parent and say, 'My son talks a great deal about your son. Perhaps you would like to come to the park with us one afternoon.' These friendships often turn into parents helping each other out with school runs, reminding each other about upcoming events and even handing down uniforms that younger children can use.
- Get involved with the school events, attend all sporting events, school concerts and sports days if at all possible.
- Read and keep school newsletters.

- Assist with homework and encourage your children to stretch themselves. But *encourage*, do not *push*. Reward achievements and congratulate your child on achievement – like a gold star for good behaviour.

- Don't turn into a pushy parent and force your child to do things they don't want to, such as extracurricular activities.

- Watch out for unusual or negative behaviour patterns and take action.

- Ensure you and your wife put the post-divorce anger behind you when it comes to education issues and possible problem areas.

- Always give positive reinforcement.

- Ensure you have a routine during the school week and stick to it, especially with issues such as breakfast time, getting to school, pick-up times, dinner times, homework time, play time and bedtime, as well as curfews.

- Be prepared for teenage angst and adopt a positive approach to dealing with it.

Chapter 13

Keeping Your Children Healthy

No matter what age your children, all parents worry when they get ill and so in this chapter I will look at the best ways to keep your children healthy when they are with you. A positive and healthy lifestyle will prevent sickness and ensure your child is happy and content.

When it comes to your children's health, there is one key rule: if you feel worried or feel you cannot cope with any form of symptom or accident, call the doctor immediately. Do not try and be a super-dad. If the solution is not obvious, act immediately. Better to be safe than sorry.

How to raise healthy children

Raising healthy children revolves around nine key factors:

- Good nutrition.

- Proper sleep patterns.

- Regular check-ups and recognising milestones, especially in the early years.

- Know your children's doctors, health care visitors and specialists and keep a record of their visits, letters and phone numbers.

- Staying safe and being taught home, play and road safety.

- Regular exercise.

- Hygiene, including food hygiene.

- Childhood illnesses and symptoms – knowing what to expect and how to diagnose.

- Your household first aid kit.

Nutrition

Children and food is a topic that has already been covered in depth (see pages 97–119). Key points to remember, however, are:

- Plan your menus for when your children are with you and shop accordingly to ensure a balanced nutritional intake.

- Read the labels on the food and check salt and sugar levels.

- Avoid sweet and sugary drinks and encourage your children to drink water instead of fizzy drinks.

- Eat with your children and eat the same meals as them.

- Ensure they have three proper meals a day – breakfast is particularly important – and limit snacks between meals to healthy options.

- Limit treats. Do not fall into the trap set by children who say, 'Mum lets us have chocolate,' or 'Mum always takes us to McDonald's.' Guilt then tricks you into doing what the child wants. Be strong and allow such treats only occasionally.

- Also many parents after divorce tend to use treats like chocolate or sweets as a way of over-compensating or preventing tantrums. Try not to fall into that trap as it creates bad habits.

Remember: a healthy child with good nutritional values is a happy child.

Proper sleep patterns

As you should realise by now, routine is critical. Eating nutritionally balanced meals at the same time each day keeps your children happy and well fed, and it is the same with sleep.

If a child, particularly a young child, does not have a proper sleep routine he or she will be more susceptible to illness. During sleep, a child's body repairs damaged cells, builds a healthy immune system and assists their growth hormones.

Children's brains need a rest, too. The number of things that young children learn each day is vast and they can become overloaded if they do not get proper rest. So ensure you have a positive bedtime routine that includes bath time, reading a book and lights out on time each night.

As for how much sleep a child needs, that can vary from child to child. Talk to other parents with children of a similar age and see what the average is and work out a time for your children. Research suggests the following:

- Newborns – they sleep most of the day although averaging around 16 hours. However, they will probably only go down for three or four hours at a stretch, due to feeding patterns.

- Six months – babies at this age will sleep 10–12 hours a night, with 2–4-hour naps during the day.

- One year – expect your child to sleep between 10 and 12 hours, with a nap during the day.

- Toddlers – they require 10–11 hours a night. However, their daytime nap needs to be phased out by three-and-a-half.

- School age – a child needs around 10 hours sleep a night. Children up to about eight years old will tend to wake at the same time each morning, no matter what time they go down at night – and it is often early.

- Teenage years – you will find yourself wondering if they are sleeping too much, but a good eight or nine hours is needed.

Be strict with bedtime routines and you will have a happy, energised child ready to fight off infections and illness.

Sleep safety

It is important to create a safe sleeping environment for your child to maintain orderly sleep patterns

Whatever cot or bed your child sleeps in, buy it from a reputable shop and check that it confirms to current safety regulations, such as the CE mark.

If your child has graduated to a bed, it often helps to put one side of the bed against the wall and a safety bar along the other side, to prevent the child rolling out. However, do not put the bed next to a radiator or other heater. Equally, do not put it directly under the window, blinds, electrical appliances or cords hanging from cupboards or ceilings.

Also ensure your child's room is safe. For very young children, this includes child safety locks on cupboards and drawers, and slow-closing toy box lids.

Top sleeping tips

● Establish a routine.

● If problems occur, do not expect your ex to handle it. Discuss it with her and if she will not listen, take action yourself.

● Deal head on with bed-wetting and monster mania. They may be indicators of a child's underlying fears and anxieties.

● Develop positive reinforcements for positive behaviour, such as star charts or special rewards.

● If your children wake from nightmares, cuddles and love work the best.

There is more on bedtime routines and training your children to go to bed on time on page 226.

Regular check-ups

In the first nine months of a child's life there are specific check-ups that they must undergo, including weekly checks with a health visitor for the first six weeks to check on growth, a month two check-up with the GP to check on feeding, sleeping habits and development, regular health clinic visits and in month eight a further GP check-up. After that it is up to parents, together with health visitors and GPs, to arrange regular check-ups, so ensure your ex-wife tells you when these are and involve yourself. These are separate, of course, from doctor's visits when the child is ill.

Immunisation

Immunisation is also an important part of your child's life. It is a hotly debated topic that needs to be discussed with your ex-wife and a clear plan agreed on. Immunisations are designed to protect your child against many illnesses, including diphtheria, tetanus, pertussis (whooping cough), polio, mumps, measles, meningitis C, rubella (German measles) and tuberculosis (TB).

Parents will be reminded when to take their child in for these immunisations. It is critical that you insist in the custody agreement that if your wife has custody or even in shared custody cases she sends you a copy of the immunisation letters. Also, ask your GP and health visitor to ensure they send you duplicates.

First years immunisation schedule	
Age	**Immunisation**
Two months	DTa/IPV/Hib* + pneumococcal vaccine**
Three months	DTa/IPV/Hib + meningitis C vaccine
Four months	DTa/IPV/Hib + meningitis C and pneumococcal vaccine
One year	Hib/meningitis C
13 months	MMR*** and pneumococcal vaccine
4–4½ years	DT/IPV

* DTaP/IPV/Hib vaccine protects against diphtheria (D), tetanus (T), pertussis (whooping cough), polio (IPV = inactivated polio vaccine) and Hib (*haemophilus influenzae* type b).

** The pneumococcal vaccine protects against pneumococcal infection that can cause diseases such as pneumonia, septicaemia and meningitis.

*** MMR protects against measles, mumps and rubella (German measles).

There are possible side effects of the vaccines and your doctor will explain. If at all possible, it is helpful for both parents to be present, not only to reassure the children but also, because of the implications for custody arrangements, you both need to be aware of possible side-effects and how to deal with them. Make sure you are aware when immunisations take place, even if you are not there.

Health milestones

As a parent you should also be aware of the health milestones by which doctors and health care workers measure the development of your child. It is important that both parents are aware of them, because prompt identification of a child not meeting a milestone may help in early diagnosis of a health issue. For you as a father, watching and knowing what to expect can be an exciting part of your children's time with you. Note that I have only listed some of the milestones to look out for. You should talk to your own GP for more detailed guidance.

Age-related skills

Up to one month	Primitive reflexes, the baby sucks objects placed near his mouth, can see objects around 30 cm/12 in in front of him. By three weeks he can move, so watch out.
Two months	Smiling starts. Follows objects with his eyes. Starts reaching for things and cooing.
Three months	Starts following objects and searching for sounds. Holds objects in his hand. Rolls from front to back.
Four months	More control of his head and arms. Laughs. Can see across the room.
Five months	Enjoys tickling. Starts playing with his own fingers.

Six months	Sits with your help. Starts baby-talking to toys. Can attempt drinking from a cup if you hold it.
Seven months	Food and hunger awareness develops. Recognises mum and dad as very important and cries when a stranger comes close.
Eight months	Crawling attempts start. Vowel and consonant sounds start
Nine months	Waves goodbye. Anxiety about being separated from mum and dad increases. Sits unsupported.
Ten-twelve months	Walking starts by using furniture. Knows his name. Starts feeding himself with his finger. *Dada* and *mama* start being used.
By fifteen months	Starts copying words. Starts crawling up stairs. Can hold a cup and drink.
Eighteen months	Temper tantrums are common, can run and is possessive over toys.
Two years	Will follow and copy you. Can kick a ball. Feeding himself at meal times. Starting to construct sentences.
Three years	Know how old he is and what sex he is. Can ride a tricycle and dress himself. Can repeat rhymes. Might start to play with imaginary friends.
Four years	Toilet trained and able to use the toilet on his own. Can speak accurately and tell a basic story, throw a ball, and easily dress and undress himself.

| Five years | School increases writing and drawing skills. Can count and name colours. Domestic role-play is prominent. |
| Six years | Deciduous (milk/baby) teeth start falling out. Dancing and playing a musical instrument are possible. Reading and writing skills have developed. Likes organised sport. |

Cognitive development

As a dad, it is important that you understand these milestones because you will be able to help your children with their creativity and problem-solving skills:

Age	Development stage
Up to two years	This is a rapid learning curve as your baby uses sight, touch and sucking to learn. He is on the slow process of discovering himself and his environment. You will notice him slowly expanding the distance he crawls and the things he touches. At around four months, your child suddenly realises things are permanent and do not disappear when he cannot see them. Games like 'peek-a-boo' or 'where's baby?' help develop the imagination, which should be encouraged. Hide a favourite toy under your jumper and magically make it appear.
Two to four years	This is 'me, me, me,' time: my toy, my dolly, as the child grasps ownership concepts. By three, language skills are developing so start reading to him. Picture books are great because you can name something and ask the child to point to it and then congratulate him, great for the

	imagination and social creativity. Your child may develop faster in this area if he attends nursery.
Four to seven years	At four years of age it is no longer 'me, me, me,' but conversations start to occur. Your child knows about 1,500 words and by age five about 2,000 words. There are lots of 'why' questions being asked and your child will expect an answer. To help him develop skills, use jigsaws, train sets, play dough, dressing up boxes. Enact a favourite story and join in yourself. He loves visiting zoos, aquariums and museums. By seven children consider themselves grown up and school homework starts becoming part of their life, so offer to help and check what they are doing.

Social skills

As a parent, developing social skills in your child is important, everything from manners to the ability to behave properly in various situations, so be aware of these milestones.

Age	Developmental stage
Up to two years	This is the period where social development between parent and child is most focused. By three months you can tell if your baby is happy or sad by facial expressions. By five months he may be clingy because he knows how much he needs his parents. At one year the baby starts demanding his own way, but openly displays affection to you.
Two to four years	Your child becomes more independent and there will be temper tantrums as they reach the 'terrible twos'. At three, the child is more aware of other children and enjoys

	co-operative play by sharing roles. He might have a special friend. By four he will have more friends.
Five to seven years	School age means interacting with more children, so ensure your child is prepared for this. A best friend will probably appear and the teachers will assist you in helping the child develop social values. School can be scary so keep an eye on your child and talk regularly to them about it.

As a parent remember these milestones are simply guides. It is important you understand what should be expected at various ages and actively encourage your child's imagination, be there to help them develop their verbal skills and help them develop friendships, and ease the transitions from pre-school to nursery to school. As a divorced dad, you have to pay extra attention to these milestones to ensure the impact of the divorce is not adversely affecting your children. If you feel it is, talk to their mother, their teachers and friends. Each child is different, so if yours do not hit the milestone at an exact age do not panic, but remember that early identification and resolution of potential problems is important.

Staying safe

Getting divorced and setting up your new home means you must re-evaluate its safety for a child of any age. The dangers to your children change with age; boiling water might not be a danger to nine-year-olds, but cycling with their mates could be.

If you are on your own it can be difficult to keep an eye on the children while tying to keep your household together. But your priority must be: children's safety first.

In the house

For children under five, it is important to fix child safety locks on cupboards and drawers containing chemicals, medicines and other potentially dangerous items, such as knives.

Stair gates are important, particularly when children are learning to walk, or when you are looking after them and want to ensure they remain in the same area as you.

Ensure your windows have locks on them and catches that allow them to open only a portion of the way to prevent falls or accidents. Windows and glass doors, including the shower, should have shatterproof glass or be fitted with safety film.

Also ensure any tables or shelves with sharp edges are either covered with foam or curved off. Falling furniture is a big risk for small children, so make sure that the wobbly book shelf is fixed and cannot fall on to a small child trying to climb. Make sure curtain pulls and string on blinds are up high, as young children can get tangled or strangled.

Put a non-slip mat in the bath for bath time.

Teach children about the dangers of hot ovens and hot water taps as soon as they understand the concept. Use guards on the front of the stove to reduce the risks of burns and scalds from pots and pans.

Children's toys

Check your children's toys regularly. If a toy breaks and cannot be repaired and has sharp parts, throw it away.

Be careful with toys that have lengths of string.

If your child has a rocking horse or wheeled toy they can ride on, make sure you are always around to supervise.

Dolls and stuffed animals should be washed regularly because they can harbour germs. Turn the task into a fun game and bonding session by letting them help give the toys a bath. Cot toys can also be soiled, so wash them regularly.

Outside issues

Children love to play in gardens. However, they also love fairy stories and can be attracted to poisonous berries, so check your garden and remove any potentially dangerous plants. Put up a home poison chart in your garage or garden shed and keep one in the kitchen.

All outbuildings, including the garage, should be kept locked unless an adult is there. Boxes are often stacked high in storage rooms and items just thrown in, and while this makes a great place to play hide and seek, it is also a great place to get hurt.

Keep garden tools and garden chemicals locked in a shed. All items should be stored properly, with all candles, matches and lighting fluids stored up high.

Small children should not have access to ponds. Where possible, make sure that children cannot wander on to the road by having gates and fences.

Car and road safety

Each year thousands of children are killed and injured by being hit by cars or involved in car accidents.

Teach your child road safety and never to cross the road without an adult being present until they are old enough.

Ensure your child has a properly fitted car seat appropriate for their age and size. In Britain, for instance, it is the driver's responsibility to ensure that any child under 14 years of age is properly restrained. Swapping child seats can become a pain, so consider two sets.

Play safety

Playing in parks and going on hikes is fun, but it is important that you set guidelines for acceptable behaviour. Always watch your children and carry a first aid kit in your car.

At home, if you have a swing or slide in your garden put outdoor rubber matting underneath it or a thick layer of child-friendly sand or wood chips, so that if there is a fall the possibility of the child hurting themselves is limited.

If you have a sand pit, fill it with special child-friendly play sand, not builder's sand.

When bike riding – even on a tricycle – use helmets as it establishes a 'safety first' concept at an early stage.

Exercise

Healthy eating and sleeping are critical to a healthy child, and so is exercise. Statistics show that the UK's childhood obesity rates are increasing at alarming rates and that many UK children never play outside every week. That is why as a dad when the children are with you must involve them in exercise. This can be anything from simply dancing in the house, walking to school or the shops or organised events like ballet or soccer.

Here are some suggestions of ways to incorporate both planned and unplanned exercise into your child's life:

● Walking to school with you.

● Dancing to the radio.

● Gentle wrestling and rumbling on the floor.

● Walking to the shops.

● Hikes.

● Gardening.

● Bike riding.

● Kite flying.

● Swimming.

● Soccer, tennis or other sport.

● Ballet or other dance.

● Walking around the supermarket instead of sitting them in the trolley.

● Going to the park.

There are heaps of other ideas and even if you only manage 15 minutes a day of outside exercise, you will be increasing your child's chance of good health and reducing their chances of falling ill.

Proper hygiene

As a parent it is important that you introduce a routine of hygiene into your child's life from an early age, because it will prevent illness and help the immune system in its fight against infections. Keeping your children healthy does not rely on stopping children getting dirty and having fun or washing every surface in your house with bleach. It is simply making sure that what goes in their bodies is clean and healthy.

Routine hygiene comprises:

● Teaching your children basic hygiene and ensuring they develop good habits.

● Teaching your children the difference between clean and dirty and what germs can do to them.

● Constantly reminding them by leading the way whether at home or out in public to practise proper hygiene.

Teaching your child about germs

Explain in simple terms that there are tiny things that can make you ill, that you cannot see but that can get into your body by someone sneezing or coughing, or by you touching dirty things, or by not washing your hands after using the toilet and before eating. If it is easier, make up a story about the very tiny bad animal that makes people sick unless they do certain things.

Teaching your children to keep themselves clean

From an early age, starting from the time your child is a baby, wash your hands with them and as they get older ensure they do it regularly themselves. I suggest a hand-washing chart with stickers encouraging children to win stickers for washing their hands and face when they wake up, before meals, before snacks, after they have used the toilet, when they have been outside, after playing with animals or visiting someone who is sick.

Get into a routine that before every meal everyone washes their hands. Double check before you start your meal.

When away from home on picnics or journeys, try getting a small container of hand sanitiser (available from chemists) or wet wipes to clean your hands before eating.

Make nightly baths and showers a routine. From an early age, teach children the importance of washing their private parts. I call it wash your 'bits and pits' and from the age of one talked to my child when I was doing this and as toddlers in the bath let them do it. Little boys who are uncircumcised may need to be shown how to clean their penis properly, so do not be shy. Start from an early age and be open about this. Similarly, little girls need to be told to wash their private parts from front to back, so that germs from faecal matter that can cause urinary tract infections do not enter the body.

Food preparation

If, like me, you make cakes and cook with your children, ensure they wash their hands before you start. Follow proper food hygiene rules, including washing fruit and vegetables; in fact, that is a great job for young children to do.

Prevent food poisoning or the spread of germs by following these guidelines:

- Use paper towels to clean down surfaces. Many washing-up cloths are a breeding ground for bugs.

- Do not use the same knives and chopping boards for raw meat and fish as for bread, cheese and ham. Always wash utensils after being used on raw meats.

- Sterilise washing-up sponges in the microwave for 15 seconds.

- Wash tea towels regularly, as damp cloths breed bacteria.

- Keep surfaces, including high chairs, fridge doors and bin handles, clean and involve your children in the cleaning. For older children, draw up a rota.

- Cook food thoroughly.

- If you reheat previously cooked food that has been in the fridge, only do it once and ensure that it is piping hot before you eat it.

- Do not open cans of food and then put half the can in the fridge. Either put the contents into a sealed, plastic container and date it or throw it out.

Brushing teeth

Proper hygiene also includes teeth. Lots of parents fail to put enough effort into encouraging their children to clean their teeth after meals because they know they are just the baby set. Do not do that.

Ensure you get your child into a routine of cleaning their teeth in the morning and at night. You can get some great children's toothbrushes and toothpastes so let the younger children choose their own. Clean your teeth with them.

Add a column for teeth cleaning to your hand-washing reward chart and talk to your children about things that are good and bad for their teeth.

To teach a young child how to brush, let them watch you brush your teeth a few times and then let them play act cleaning your teeth.

Use a child's toothbrush and toothpaste. Small children should only use a pea-sized amount of toothpaste; children's toothpaste has a taste that is better suited to younger palates. Stand the child on a step so they can reach the basin and gently start brushing or massaging the teeth with the brush. Talk about what you are doing, brush for around a minute and ask them to spit and then using a small cup get them to take a small mouthful and spit again.

You must be persistent with teeth. Often they get forgotten, so make sure you supervise the teeth-cleaning and help them as much as possible. Also take them to the dentist regularly, so they are not scared by the experience.

Common childhood illnesses and symptoms

Every parent worries about their children falling ill. So far, we have discussed how to keep them healthy. Now it is time to learn about the most common childhood illnesses and their symptoms and treatment.

The basic rule to follow as parents is that if your child is very ill, it is in their best interests to avoid moving them between homes. Whichever home they are in when they become ill should be the home the child stays at, even if they are due back with the other parent, until they are feeling better. This also avoids spreading germs, especially if your other partner has a stepfamily and children with her new partner.

Symptoms that may indicate a child is unwell

Children, as we all know, can sometimes complain of feeling sick to get extra attention or avoid doing things they do not want to do, such as going to school, taking an exam or helping tidy up. As a dad, it is important that you listen carefully when a child complains of feeling unwell and learn to recognise when they are play acting and when the complaint is real.

The following is a list of symptoms that you should look out for and always take seriously:

- Listlessness and sleeping more than normal.

- High temperature above 39°C/100°F.

- Runny nose.

- Swollen glands (feel the side of the neck just below the ear for lumps).

- Vomiting.

- Complaints of a sore, itchy or spiky throat.

- Headache.

- Stomach ache – especially if the child is refusing food and continues to complain of it or shows sensitivity when the stomach is pressed.

- Blisters and rashes.

- Coughing and sneezing.

- Talking with a croaky voice.

- Wheezing or difficulty breathing.

- Earache or constantly pulling at the ear.

- Spots and reddish marks or blisters around or inside mouth.

- Spots on the face.

- Dry, itchy, red, patches on the skin.

- Complaints of itchiness around the genital area or pain when urinating.

- Dislike of bright lights.

- Crying, moaning and unusual clinginess, especially in young children.

- Balance problems or problems holding cups or toys.

- Problems going to the toilet or runny stools.

- Complaining of joint pain or a pain in a certain part of the body, such as the wrist or ankle.

Each of these can be indicators that your child is unwell, so if you feel that is the case keep them quiet and calm and ensure they have enough fluids (just water) until you are sure the symptoms are continuing.

Common ailments

This section is a guide only. The ailments are discussed in only general terms; this book is not a medical handbook. If you are worried, it is vital that you take your child directly to the doctor or hospital emergency room.

Allergies

Children can develop allergies to various foods – for example nuts, milk or shellfish – or to pets like dogs and cats. They are normally indicated by a rash or, for foods, tingling in the mouth. If you suspect an allergy you need to visit your doctor and have a range of tests done to determine what the trigger is. You then must stick to the stringent measures the doctor lays out to avoid attacks, as some allergies can cause serious illness or even death. You should be particularly cautious about introducing some foods to your child's diet, such as nuts, if it is known that the allergy is present in other family members.

Asthma

Asthma is occurring in more and more children in the UK. Symptoms include a cough without a cold, wheezing and coughing, an inability to take in breath when excited or upset, or when exposed to some allergen. If you think your child has asthma, you must consult you doctor because it can be a dangerous ailment and needs immediate treatment in the form of inhalers and steroids.

Chickenpox

It is likely your child will get chickenpox. On the first day a rash appears as small red patches about 3–4 mm/¼ in across. They can be mistaken for a mosquito bite or a spot or scratch on the face. But within a few hours of these developing, small blisters appear in the centre of these patches. During the next three or four days, further patches will appear. Some children get covered in spots, others have spots limited to various areas. The spots are very itchy, so use cool baths and calamine lotion to reduce the urge to scratch. Scratching can cause scarring. Your child is infectious from about two days before the spots appear until about five days after the last one. If you suspect your child has chickenpox, keep them at home and contact your GP for confirmation and advice.

Cold sores

These are extremely common and are caused by the herpes simplex virus. The virus causes painful blisters to appear around the lips. Children between three and five are most susceptible and often pick it up from nursery or school. Symptoms include tingling, blisters appearing and a fever or aches. See your pharmacist for child cold sore cream. Cold sores are very contagious so ensure your child washes their hands frequently and does not touch the sores. Keep toys, towels and bed linen separate until the outbreak is over.

Colds and flu

All children will get colds. It is a fact of life and usually caused by seasonal changes or by one child bringing the bug to nursery or school. Children develop immunity, so if they have been at a certain nursery for, say, a year and then they start school, they will encounter new children and new environments, so their chances of falling ill rise for a while. Symptoms include a runny nose, cough and temperature. Some children complain of aches and pains. Colds are mostly caused by viruses, so antibiotics are of no use in their treatment. However, if you are worried, see the doctor. The best way to care for the child is to keep them warm and calm, and to use paracetamol for children as directed on the packet to reduce the temperature and aches and pains. Encourage them to drink water. Keep them warm but do not let them become overheated with too many blankets or heating, and simply wait it out. If a cough develops, talk to the doctor or pharmacist about an appropriate cough syrup. There are day and night options, which will encourage the child to sleep at the right time. Keep a diary of when all medication is given. If symptoms persist, consult a doctor.

If you have been to the doctor and medication, either prescription or over-the-counter, is being used, ensure the child's mother knows about it, and at handover give her details of when the last dose was given.

Constipation

Constipation is a common problem among children. Symptoms include fewer bowel movements than normal, pain when passing their stool or dry, hard stools, tummy aches, a sore bottom, an unpleasant smell, dribbling urine and an avoidance of using the toilet. Constipation is caused by a number of factors, including: not enough fibre in the diet; not drinking enough water; drinking too much milk, behavioural factors, such as changing schools; lack of exercise; family history; or certain medicines. Encourage a greater fluid intake, more fibre in your child's diet and more exercise. Some child-friendly laxatives are available if these measures do not improve the situation. Encourage your children to use the toilet regularly and not to give up trying, because if a stool builds up it can cause enormous pain for a child. If constipation continues, see your doctor for advice.

Croup

Croup occurs in children between three and five years of age. Symptoms include a harsh cough, noisy breathing, which can sound quite frightening, and a fever. The best way to treat croup is to keep your child calm, try hot steam inhalations, sit them up so they breathe more easily and encourage them to drink lots. If it continues, see your GP.

Ear infections

Ear infections are common in young children and can cause crying and much discomfort. They are caused by a build-up in the middle ear of fluid that cannot drain away adequately. Lie the child down on their side on some extra pillows, with the painful ear uppermost. Treat the pain with paracetamol. If the earache continues for more than one day or recurs, see your doctor, as medication may be required.

Eczema

Eczema symptoms include constant scratching and you will see a dry, red and itchy rash on your child, commonly on the hands, skin folds, neck and face. It can also start off as tiny blisters. There is no cure for eczema, but you need to talk to the doctor about controlling it with a number of treatments, which include antihistamines, steroids and emollients. It can also help to wear natural fibres such as 100% cotton close to the skin, and to avoid bubble bath, fabric softener and other strongly scented products.

Food poisoning and diarrhoea

The most important thing is to rest the digestive system for 24 hours and to comfort the child, especially if they are vomiting or experiencing diarrhoea. Ensure you replace fluids lost by making them drink little but often, sticking to water only; avoid milk. Yes, they may throw it back up, but some will stay in the system. You can try rehydration powders from the chemist, but children do not always like the salty taste. Do not give your child anti-diarrhoea medication without consulting a pharmacist or doctor, as most are designed for adults only and must be supervised by a doctor. Keep an eye on the child's temperature and ensure you give them lots of cuddles. Try to take their mind off the situation by watching a DVD or reading a favourite book.

Head lice

Your children are likely to get head lice at least once in their lives and it is not due to poor hygiene on your part – lice like clean hair. All it takes is one child to bring lice into school and you have an outbreak. You can buy anti-lice shampoo over the counter from chemists, which you apply and then work through wet hair with a small-toothed comb to remove the nasty creatures and their eggs. Read the directions for use carefully before you start.

Insect bites and stings

Comfort the child and immediately establish where the bite or sting is. If the sting is still present on the skin, brush it off and apply child-friendly insect bite cream. Cold compresses will often ease the symptoms and reduce the urge to scratch. Some young children love investigating the garden and catching insects, so buy a book on insects and teach your children which are safe and which sting.

Measles

Measles are most infectious two or three days before the rash appears. The rash is blotchy and red and appears on the body and face, there will be greyish-white spots in the mouth and throat, and the child might exhibit symptoms similar to a cold. Your child will remain infectious for up to 10 days. Keep them quiet and calm. If they have a fever use paracetamol to control the temperature. Measles is a potentially serious illness, so if you suspect your child has it, you must keep them at home and contact your GP for confirmation and advice.

Minor cuts and bruises

Soothe the child and then wash the graze or cut with water. Apply a plaster or clean bandage and hold firmly for five minutes. If bleeding continues, the cut may need stitches, so see a doctor. Otherwise, just keep the dressing clean. If necessary, apply a plaster, but beware that while children love plasters and wear them like a badge of honour, the process of taking them off can be more painful than the original accident! Try soaking them off in the bath or consider a can of spray plaster. The spray seals the wound and does not need removing. Some children are allergic to plasters and you should look out for reddening or itching. If this occurs, remove the plaster immediately and if the redness is severe consult a doctor.

To prevent bruising, immediately apply a cold compress made from ice wrapped in a towel. Chemists sell gel-filled packs in the shape of animals, which can be kept in the fridge until needed. My children love them and they work effectively.

Mumps

The glands around the front and back of the neck under the ear swell up. There will be a high temperature and your child may feel pain opening their mouth. Ensure the child rests and stays in bed for as long as the temperature and swelling last. If they have a fever, use paracetamol to control the temperature. If you suspect your child has mumps, keep them at home and contact your GP for confirmation and advice.

Nose bleeds

The sight of blood can cause parents to panic, but you must keep calm so that your child feels confident in your behaviour. Remain calm, put your child in a chair or on your lap, lean them forward with their mouth open and pinch their nose below the bone for about ten minutes. Use a cold compress to wipe up the blood. You can loosely plug a nostril with tissue paper to encourage a clot to form, but beware when removing the paper that the nose bleed might start up again.

Once bleeding has stopped, sit the child up, clean them up, and avoid food or hot drinks for an hour. If the bleeding persists, see the doctor. If the nosebleed is the result of a fall or bump, watch out for signs of concussion, including listlessness, dizziness and lack of memory.

Rubella (German measles)

The child develops a rash during the first day that usually covers the body, arms and legs in small pink patches about 2–3 cm/1 in across. The rash does not itch, but the child might complain of aching joints. Your child is infectious two or three days before the rash appears and until the rash goes, which takes another five days, and should not mix with other children who have not had German measles. Women who are pregnant should keep away from children with rubella, because the illness can cause damage to unborn babies if the mother catches it. If you suspect your child has rubella, keep them at home and contact your GP for confirmation and advice.

Sprains or fractures

Determine where it hurts and what happened, then immediately apply a cold compress of ice in a towel. If the pain subsides in about ten minutes, simply keep treating with a cold compress and perhaps use paracetamol as directed on the packet. Otherwise, take the child to the doctor or emergency room, even if you think nothing is broken.

Stomach ache

Stomach aches in children are usually caused by wind, indigestion, eating their food too fast or eating too much at a party. Try a hot water bottle wrapped in a towel on their tummy in the case of indigestion, and 5 ml/1 tsp of bicarbonate of soda in half a glass of water will help. If the pain goes on longer than eight hours, go to the doctor. Most stomach aches will be painful when the stomach is gently pressed. Try distracting the child and press their stomach to check for sensitivity; this may help diagnosing the real tummy aches.

Sunburn

Letting your children get sunburn is irresponsible. Always use good-quality, high-factor sunscreen and re-apply regularly. Try spray-on sunscreen; some have a colour in them so you can see where it is applied, then the colour fades in a few minutes.

But if the worst happens and the child is burnt, first of all sponge them with lukewarm water or give them a cool bath. Then apply either calamine lotion or a child-friendly after-sun cream. Paracetamol will help with the pain but only as directed on the packet. Cuddles and keeping the child calm are important. Children who are old enough to understand should be reminded about the importance of adequate sun protection lotion. With younger ones it is your responsibility.

First aid kit

You should have a first aid kit and everyone in the household should know where it is kept. You should also have a mini kit for your car. Check it regularly to ensure that any medicines have not gone out of date and that supplies are topped up. Your kit should include:

- Plasters – you can buy them with children's characters on.

- Antibacterial wipes.

- Thermometer – electric thermometers are quicker than glass ones, or for youngsters you can buy a strip that you press on the forehead.

- Bandages, gauzes, tape and a sling – and learn how to put it on!

- Scissors.

- Tweezers.

- Safety-pins.

- Child cough syrup – one for dry coughs and one for chesty coughs, available in day and night time options.

- Childhood paracetamol or ibuprofen.

- Cold compress gel pack – kept in the fridge.

- Calamine lotion.

- Sunscreen – a high factor for young skins.

- Insect bite cream.

- Anti-itch cream.

- Germ foam for washing hands in cars.

- Surgical gloves.

You can purchase home kits from most chemists or online, and kits for the car are available from some motor stores.

First aid course

As a new hands-on divorced dad, I strongly recommended that you do a short first aid course. Contact your local council or St John Ambulance for information or ask at your GP's surgery. You should also invest in a basic first aid book. It pays to be prepared, particularly now that you are on your own with your children. You can no longer pool your knowledge with your wife, so make the effort to know what to do in an emergency. This includes:

● How to resuscitate a child.

● How to give CPR to a child.

● How to put a child in the recovery position.

● Treating a child for shock.

● Coping with severe bleeding.

Doctors, health workers and specialists

As a divorced dad, it is important that you are involved in all the decisions about your children's health and well-being, and this should include developing a good relationship with their doctor, medical specialists and health visitors. You can do this by:

● Knowing the names of all your children's health care professionals and being able to talk knowledgably about their needs and health.

● Being present at all major check-ups.

● Being present at immunisations.

● Being copied in on all health visitor, doctor and consultant letters if you are unable to attend appointments in person.

TOP TIPS ON CHILD HEALTH CARE

- If in doubt, call a doctor – never take chances.
- Focus on keeping your children healthy through a routine of good food, sound sleep and exercise.
- Proper hygiene is critical to a healthy child.
- Be able to recognise your child's milestones and understand what they mean.
- Communicate with your ex. For instance, if you have been giving cough medicine to your child, your ex needs to know when the last dose was and how much.
- Don't be frightened about health issues. The key is keeping your child healthy. You should not expect to become an instant expert on every aspect of child health; learn as you go along.
- Get to know your children's doctors. Learn when to call them and when to treat your children yourself.
- Make sure you are aware of symptoms that could indicate your child is getting sick.
- Maintain fluid levels of sick children.
- If administering medication, keep a diary of when each dose was given, what and how much. Pass on this information at handover.
- Learn to control your child's temperature when ill by using analgesics, but do not over-use them.
- Ensure you have a proper first aid kit and regularly dispose of out-of-date medicines.
- Take a first-aid course.
- Keep a file or diary of your child's illnesses.

CHAPTER 14

Taking Children on Holiday

T he details of the holidays you can take with your children will depend on the custody arrangement you have agreed with your ex. For example, in the UK, it is common that courts award half of the school holidays to each parent. How that is split up depends on the orders negotiated.

Planning holidays with your children

If you are a working divorced dad, lodge your holiday applications early to coincide with the children's school holidays. There will probably be lots of other parents at your workplace wanting the same time off, so get in early and plan for the entire year or you might miss out.

Your budget will affect where you go. A holiday does not have to mean an expensive trip abroad. You could simply holiday at home and do daytrips to discover areas of your city or county you have never visited before.

Schools generally discourage family holidays taken during term time as they are deemed to be disruptive and detrimental to your children's education. However, there is provision for you to apply to take your child out of school for a certain length of time each year for a holiday, if you complete the forms and the head teacher gives permission. Many parents choose this option because holidays are cheaper outside of school holiday time or because they cannot get school holiday time off at their work. If your children are at boarding school, this will also have implications.

If you are subject to court orders, you might not be allowed to take your children out of the country/town without the mother's permission, so advance planning regarding permission and passports is essential.

Ultimately, and particularly if your children are under six, you will be the person that makes the choice of what to do on their school holidays. However, it is important to talk about the event in positive terms.

Ideas for holidays for young children

Weigh up different types of holidays. An all-inclusive holiday can sometimes be less expensive than a holiday in your own country. If you are choosing to holiday at a resort, ensure it is child friendly, check its rating with travel agencies and ask your children if it is a place they would like to visit.

Even if money is tight, you can have a great holiday by visiting friends, particularly if they have children the same age as yours. They will be able to help you to plan a nice itinerary of fun things to do in their town.

Many divorces see former partners moving to a new town away from the grandparents, so taking children to visit them or other relatives is an easy and inexpensive option. It also reminds the children of the importance of extended family.

Other options include a trip to the seaside staying in a child-friendly bed-and-breakfast; staying on a farm to see and do countryside activities; camping or caravanning.

Keep the holiday relatively short if it is in a bed-and-breakfast, longer if you are staying with friends or family. A collapsible travel cot is useful for babies.

Wherever you go, if you have more than one child, try and take another adult friend or family member with you. It helps to have an extra pair of hands so that if, for instance, you take one child swimming, there is someone to care for the other children while you are in the pool.

Don't forget to pack a couple of familiar items, such as a blanket, some books or a favourite toy.

Ideas for holidays for children aged 6 to 12

Children of this age will start developing their own ideas on what type of holiday they want. Ask for their input, but make sure they know that you are working to a budget. This is the age you can start taking them on longer trips, take them overseas for holidays or visit places like Disneyland or go on family adventure holidays that involve package deals such as horse riding or rock climbing.

If you are planning a trip to a hotel, ensure the facilities are child friendly and that there are activities nearby that will interest your child. There is no point in choosing a lovely hotel if it is nowhere near any tourist destinations, such as zoos, aquariums and museums.

If you are going overseas, you must give the children's mother suitable notice and arrange to text or e-mail her an update part way through the holiday. Travelling overseas means passports, visas and health insurance and other documents must be done on time. Check with your travel advisor if you are travelling to the Far East or Africa in case certain inoculations may be required and you will have to prepare in advance.

When it comes to packing, check the temperature of your destination and make sure that the clothes that you take for your children will be suitable; it might be winter here, but summer where you are going. Give each child a small travel bag on wheels and let them pack their bag and then check they have what they need. This helps keep them involved in the pre-holiday preparation.

Take some books, holiday board games and other items for the journey or for use during the holiday. If your budget stretches to it, I recommend a mini portable DVD for the children. I have two and they are brilliant on long car journeys or train trips.

Be prepared for delays at airports, train stations and bus stations so always have a bag with you with activities the children can entertain themselves with while they wait. Again, consider taking a friend or family member along to help out.

Holidays for teenagers

As always, teenagers are a different kettle of fish. Talk to them about what they would like to do well in advance and remember they may have to spend part of their holidays preparing for exams. They may also ask to take a friend along, so work out if your budget can afford that. The same general advice applies for teens as for 6–12-year-olds.

Involve teenagers in the selection, and if you are planning a trip abroad bring home books about the country to which you are travelling to get them excited. Perhaps you could ask them to use the internet to research different things the family can do.

One option is to use an exchange group that offers teens the chance to holiday with a family overseas and you play host to that family's teen. Obviously you will need to vet the organisation and talk to parents who have allowed their children to do this activity.

You will have to give teenagers a little more flexibility on holiday, but make sure you discuss curfews and warn them about the dangers of going out in areas they do not know.

Getting there

Yes, this is a case of planes, trains and automobiles.

Using your car

This can be quite a tough option even with two drivers, but now that you are on your own, it can be even harder. Consider taking an adult friend or relative with you on long trips, so you can share looking after the children and take turns driving.

Take into account the type of car you have. If you have had to downsize after your divorce, you could consider hiring or borrowing a larger vehicle for the holiday, to give everyone more space and make the journey more comfortable for you as driver and for the children as passengers.

For young children, ensure you have the correct type of car seat properly fitted. There are some seats that flick back a little when they fall asleep to make long journeys more comfortable. Do not just wait until you think the child is too big for the seat;

check their weight and the restrictions on the car seat.

Older children can help to plan part of the trip. Give each child a map of where you could stop along the way or what activities they might like to do at the destination and they can tick off their choices. They will not complain about the distance.

Stop frequently. The driver needs to take a break and children do too and it also helps break the journey.

Some children are prone to car sickness. Limit the time they spend reading as this can make it worse, while if they have a view out of the window, it limits car sickness. You can also ask your local pharmacist for over-the-counter car sickness remedies, which I suggest you keep in the car at all times.

To relieve the monotony:

- Consider investing in in-car DVD players for the children – these are portable DVD players that fit over the back of the front seat so children in the back seat can view them.

- Personal CD or MP3 players for older children – but remember long-term use of earphones listening to loud music can damage hearing.

- Create a travel diary created with a list of things the children need to tick off when they see them, e.g. certain landmarks or animals – if they tick them all, they get a treat.

- Sing-a-longs – make sure you have a ready supply of children's CDs to sing to.

- Audio books – a huge range of books are available read on CD or cassette and children love listening to them.

- Surprises – gift wrap a couple of toys, games or books and reward your children with a surprise if they have been patient or helpful. Small bags filled with a treat to eat, some stickers and a toy can go a long way toward passing extra miles.

- Making memories – older children are often whizzes at using camcorders, so get them to tape the journey for family posterity. Even the worst road trips will be memories to laugh about later, so bring a camera along and let the children take some pictures. You will see your outing from a whole new perspective!

- Road games – I spy. Can you see a red car? Who can spot the most animals? Licence plate bingo – they all help to make the time go quicker.

- Do not forget the snacks – pack an assortment to keep the children from getting hungry or thirsty between meals.

Flying

Air travel has its unique advantages (speed) and challenges (you cannot stop, no matter what happens). For happier skies, try the following.

Prepare your children. If they have never flown, turn it into an adventure. Airlines seat parents with children first, so use this time wisely to settle often over-excited children. Most airlines have special travel packs for children. On long-haul flights that offer meal options, select a meal your children will like. Pre-selected meals are handed out first and hungry children often cannot wait for the trolley to reach them. Consider requesting bulkhead seats, which face on to the divider walls.

Children under two can fly on a parent's lap, i.e. without a seat of their own, but many people feel that for maximum safety babies should occupy car seats when flying. If you can afford to buy a seat on the plane for your baby, it is money well spent.

Find out what baby equipment you can take as checked baggage. Even if you do not use your car seat on the plane, you may need it at your destination. Take a collapsible buggy for toddlers, with a buggy board as well if you have another small child so that they can both be pushed.

Check with your travel agent and the airport as to what you can take on to the plane as hand luggage. Recent terrorist alerts mean restrictions have been put in place, but they vary, so check before you pack. If possible, use a backpack and ensure your children each have a carry-on backpack with items they will need. Children with their own seats will have their own baggage and hand baggage allowance, allowing you to combine your allowance for bulky items like buggies.

Backpacks or courier bags are great because not only do they hold a lot, but they also leave your hands free to carry your baby and other paraphernalia. You will probably want to keep your money and passport in a waist pouch or other secure place, but pretty much everything else can go in the pack. You will be glad to have it at your destination, too.

If you have a long flight, think ahead about sleeping arrangements on the plane by ensuring you have your child's favourite blanket or neck pillow or stuffed animal.

Two other tips: take a portable DVD player with a stock of films. Some of the budget carriers do not offer in-flight films. Make sure, too, that you have vital items in your hand luggage in case your bags go astray.

Trains

Trains can be a great way to travel. Young children love the chance to ride the 'roaring dragon' and it allows you to take more luggage. Also, railway stations are normally in the middle of the town or city, unlike airports, so you are spared the dreaded transfers that can add extra hours to your journey.

The earlier you book your rail tickets, the cheaper they are likely to be, and always ask if there are any family concessions. Family rail cards can save their own cost on long journeys, or if you do a lot of rail travel. Some train companies have family carriages that might offer films, games and extra tables. In any case, try to sit in a section that has a table, because this gives you more space and the children can spread out their toys and games.

If your journey is around eight hours long, try a sleeper train. I am a big fan; you get your own cabin and bed, two bunks to a cabin, and you can get interconnecting cabins. It is a great adventure and if you book far enough in advance you can get cheap fares. An added bonus is that you save on accommodation the other end, because you have slept in you own bunk bed on the journey there.

During the journey, keep your children amused in any of the ways suggested on page 188.

Don't forget to pack food, but the joy of train travel for children is often a visit to the restaurant car.

Holidays and your ex

Don't turn holidays into a competition. They are not about the fact that you might be able to afford a better holiday than your wife can; it is about having a good time with your children.

If you are going out of the country, you will need your ex-wife's approval and should ask her in good time. She may ask to see the itinerary and contact details for you while you are away, so give her your mobile number and that of the hotel where you are staying. Send her a text to say you have arrived safely and then send an update halfway through the holiday. If an emergency occurs, ensure you tell your wife immediately.

Encourage your children to write a postcard to their mother and to buy her a gift. This shows the children that you respect her and that it is all right for them to think of her while you are away.

Illness while on holiday

Be prepared for anything and take a first aid kit containing basic medicines with you, such as diarrhoea remedies and children's liquid painkillers (see page 181). You should always take out holiday insurance, but this is particularly important if you are travelling overseas. If you are travelling within Europe you should also take with you a European Health Insurance Card (EHIC) for each member of your party, including the children. This plastic card replaces the old E111 paper document and entitles the holder to reduced cost, sometimes free, medical care in most European countries.

Once you arrive at your destination, check out the location of the nearest hospital with an emergency room, chemist, and emergency call-out doctors.

Minimise the risk of holiday tummy bugs by making sure that your children wash any fruit and vegetables they buy at markets, and wash their hands before and after meals. Try pocket hand sanitiser gel for when you are out and about on picnics. Do not be too adventurous in the food stakes; keep it simple because upset stomachs can ruin a holiday.

TOP TIPS FOR A SUCCESSFUL HOLIDAY

- Plan your holidays well in advance.
- Consult the children.
- Decide on a budget and stick to it.
- Ensure your ex is aware of your plans.
- Consider taking a friend or family adult member to help you if you are alone and have more than one child.
- Research your destination and determine the best mode of transport.
- Ensure younger children take a favourite toy/blanket or pillow.
- Portable DVD players are a godsend.
- Never travel without an emergency holiday bag and an emergency first aid kit.
- Ensure your children have the inoculations required if travelling overseas.
- The most important rule is to have fun.
- Have a plan for rainy and poor weather days.

CHAPTER 15

Introducing Your New Partner to Your Children

Ａs a divorced dad, you might find you spend all your time working hard and caring for your children in your free time. If all your friends are married, then suddenly you are the odd one out and invitations can dry up because you are no longer part of a couple. Divorce can also see friends split, if they take sides. If you are part of a divorced family in which everyone has moved to a new town, making new friends, let alone meeting a potential new partner, may seem overwhelming.

Start by simply making new friends among your work colleagues, by joining a sports club or taking an adult education course. Get to know other parents at your children's school, then organise play dates and invite both parents to your house or the park. Accept all party invitations that your children receive that fall on your days, and mix and mingle. Get involved in school activities, such as fêtes or school repair days. Other places to meet new people are church groups, music groups and helping a local charity.

Any of these might lead you to meet a new girlfriend, but there are other ways. Ask friends to set you up on dates, go to parties, try agencies, online dating or speed dating. Just go out and about as much as possible when you do not have the children with you.

Introducing your girlfriend to your ex-wife

Before looking at how to introduce your new partner to your children, you first need to consider how you can handle your ex-wife's reaction to her in a positive and proactive way.

The reason for this is simple. If you are adopting the business-like approach suggested earlier (see page 43), you will have to inform your ex-partner first. If she hears 'Dad's got a new girlfriend' from the children, your relationship with her can plummet. Her reaction will determine how you progress. If she becomes angry and tries to turn the children against the new woman, you will know ahead of time and be prepared. You set the standard for what you expect from her.

Starting point

If you were the cause of the divorce or break-up because you had an affair, you need to think carefully about how you now feel about the person with whom you had the adulterous relationship. You must have a clear-headed and determined approach and ask:

- Is the affair that broke up the relationship or marriage a classic, transitional relationship, a fling and a reaction to a marriage that was already failing for a range of reasons and is not long term; or

- Is this really the person you want your children to meet and a person whom you feel will become your significant other?

People often feel terrified about being single, especially after being in a long-term relationship. But do not rush into a new relationship too soon simply because you do not want to be single. Often you need to be single for a while to give yourself time to recover and the children time to adjust to their new relationship with you.

The situation can also be difficult if your wife had an affair that broke up the marriage. In this case, she is more likely to move the man whom she had the affair with straight into her home and the lives of your children. You are left to deal with the knowledge that:

- The man who assisted in damaging your marriage is now possibly spending more time with your children than you do.

- He is considered by your ex and her friends and family as a replacement father.

- He might be used to assist in excluding you from your children's lives.

- If your wife remarries, the children will have a stepfather and a father.

You may not have been consulted about how and when the children were introduced to this new man, a person you might not know. This means that, like any dad, you will worry about the impact on your children and their coping mechanisms.

Things to remember

It is only reasonable that after your divorce you will want someone in your life. But you have to put your children first.

No one is asking you to be a monk, but do take things slowly. Consider a couple of months of just being with yourself and your children, and coming to terms with all your new responsibilities. Your workload with the children has effectively doubled now you are on your own with them.

Your friends will probably try to set you up on dates, but take some time to think about all the reasons your marriage did not work and make a list of what you have learnt from that.

Beware the transitional or sticking plaster relationship. Often the first relationship after a divorce seems perfect, but fails miserably because you are trying for an immediate quick fix.

Telling your ex-wife first

You should stick to a range of overall guidelines when introducing a new girlfriend and possible partner or stepmother, and how you approach this depends on what phase of the divorce process you are in.

Still going through divorce

If you are going through the divorce process, consult your lawyer before telling your wife and introducing the woman to your children, as it may impact on your legal team's strategy for custody. Prepare her for this and possible malicious attack from your ex-wife and her legal team, if necessary. It happens and can be extremely traumatising.

Have her meet your lawyer if needs be, because she may have to give evidence on your behalf and your lawyers will have to explain to her what her impact is on your battle for custody. Introduce her formally to your wife via a lawyer's letter and lay out a strategy for the introduction of this woman. Your lawyer will ensure it is businesslike and benefits your case.

If your wife had an affair or perhaps did not tell you about her new partner before telling your children, or has a stream of male friends, do not stoop to her level. Set yourself high standards and stick to them.

Post-divorce

The worst thing in any post-divorce relationship between former partners is for an ex-wife to hear from her children, 'Dad's got a new girlfriend and she's fantastic.' The same applies to you; if suddenly the children start talking about a new man who is 'sleeping in mum's bed' and you have not been told, you are going to be concerned and feel disrespected, like an outsider who has been replaced as the children's father.

While after divorce each partner must respect the other's privacy, new partners are a different matter. Children need consistency and if your ex has boyfriends who come and go, or you have girlfriends who change and they all meet the children, you only create confusion and anxiety.

Even if your ex-wife is still angry and antagonistic towards you, you must be businesslike (see page 43) and write to her.

Here is a suggested letter:

Dear Jane,

As you know, I am committed to continuing a positive new approach with you when it comes to dealing with our children.

As part of that commitment I am writing to let you know I have met someone who is special to me. Julia is my girlfriend and I will be introducing her to the children. I have laid out a plan to do this so it is not confusing for the children and does not send mixed messages.

I plan to introduce Julia as a friend and have her attend a gathering of friends. I then plan a picnic with another group of friends and then a visit to my house for an hour to meet the children on an upcoming weekend. If that goes well, she will spend more time with us on my weekends.

I plan to discuss with the older children that she and I are dating and that I hope they will like her, but they should come to me if they have any concerns about her. I will also make it clear she is not a 'replacement mother'.

I am hoping for your support in this and hope you can appreciate I have taken very seriously the decision to introduce her. I am sensitive to both your emotions and my own. If you would like to meet her I would be happy to arrange an introduction at a date suitable to everyone with a clear agenda agreed beforehand.

Let me say in advance I would never try and replace you as the children's mother and I hope we can work together in a proactive way regarding this matter.

Kind regards,

John

Battle time: the ex vs. the new woman

If your businesslike approach fails when asking for the support of your ex in introducing a new partner, it is important that you understand why. Here are some reasons why your ex might refuse to help:

- She is playing the protective mother.

- She is envious that you have a new partner and she does not.

- She is jealous that while she has a new man, you could actually find a new woman in your life. This is called the Queen Bee complex.

- She is still recovering from the shock of the divorce and this is like a second-wave shock.

- She instigated the divorce and is determined to make your life miserable just because she can, and will try to turn the children against your new partner.

- She blames you for the divorce and feels you do not deserve happiness.

- She still feels guilty about the divorce and harbours the view that if her new relationship fails, you will be waiting for her in the wings.

- She is lonely, frightened and scared.

- She thinks the new girlfriend is unsuitable and fears she will harm the children in some way. Be careful here, because there have been cases where the new girlfriend, post or pre-divorce, can be seriously victimised.

- She feels that the sight of the children's father hanging out with a girlfriend like a teenager sends the wrong message. While it is OK for her to have a new partner, it is not for you. This is the 'do as I say, not as I do' attitude.

- She says the children are not ready and that you are being irresponsible or detrimental, and threatens to take you (back) to court.

- She wants to maintain some degree of control.

If you recognise three or more of the above, your ex-wife may be trying to bully you. Divorce brings out the best and worst emotional response in people. It is up to you to determine whether this negative response is simply post-divorce sadness or the bully complex at play. This complex occurs because of the following five reasons:

- Your ex-wife is still reverting to the behaviour pattern she exhibited when you were married, dictating how you behave.

- She has not accepted post-divorce that the children now have two homes, two families, and that you as their father are involved and coping.

- She is a bully or alpha female who enjoys the drama of saying no to you: again, an example of someone who has not moved on.

- She lives by two standards; she can have a new partner because whatever decision she makes is appropriate as she is the children's mother, but you cannot because she feels it is within her right to belittle your position and bully you.

- This complex is indistinctly linked to the bad ex phase.

You need to plan to protect yourself, your children and your new partner during this phase. Before you tell your children about a new partner, you should officially notify your ex-partner (see pages 196–197).

However, if you think she will respond in a negative way, write her a letter asking her what her response would be if you were to consider starting dating again and asking her for input as to how you should tell the children. Tell her you are only *considering* dating, but want her thoughts. You should either do this direct or through your lawyer. Again, keep it businesslike.

Here is an example:

> *Dear Jane,*
>
> *As you know, I am committed to creating a positive relationship with you since our divorce is now final. This is in the best interests of the children and us.*
>
> *Since the divorce I have remained single and have not been seeing anyone. I am considering dating again and would like your input. Naturally I will date when you have the children. Then, if I find myself in a serious relationship I will notify you that I intend to introduce the new woman to the children and how I plan to do this.*
>
> *I am asking for your input out of respect and my commitment to a more businesslike relationship with you. I have no intention of ever replacing you as the children's mother. If you have any objections or requests, please reply via e-mail or letter.*
>
> [If your ex is single still, add the following:]
>
> *As you are still single I would like to take this opportunity to ask you, out of respect, to inform me as I have just informed you when you start dating again and plan to introduce the children to a new boyfriend. Naturally, if you'd like me to take the children on nights you have them but have been invited out I am happy to oblige, as I feel it is important that we support each other in moving on with our lives.*
>
> *Kind regards,*
>
> *John*

Her response to the letter allows you to gauge her likely response to a new woman in your life and your children's lives. If she does not respond, try again. If there is no response the second time, simply write and say you take her non-response as an indication that she has no issues with you dating and possibly introducing a new partner to the children.

If she does respond but in a negative fashion, carefully analyse the letter and try to match her response to one of the points listed on page 198, as it gives you a better idea of how to deal with her. Consider seeking the advice of a counsellor, as you do not want the children upset by the situation.

What can your ex do to prevent or sabotage the introduction of a new partner?

The first thing she can do is poison the children against your new partner. Talk to your children and help them understand that it is their decision if they like your new friend, not their mum's or yours. If your children report back to you that their mother is talking negatively to them about your new girlfriend, ask her to stop, either in person or by letter. Failing that, involve your lawyer. Most importantly, talk to the children and let them make up their own minds. Listen to them, let them know you do not want to hurt their mum but that your new friend is nice.

Prepare your new girlfriend, as it is possible your ex-wife could launch an attack against her, making false accusations, and during a divorce phase this can be very difficult. I know of cases where ex-wives have claimed new girlfriends are drug addicts, alcoholics, gamblers or simply 'sad slags', when in fact they are good, hardworking and responsible people. You and your new girlfriend have to be ready to defend yourselves against these claims. At its extreme, this could mean sworn statements.

Your ex might try to limit your access to your children once you have a new partner. Discuss this with your legal advisor. I had to ask my team whether my new partner was likely to hinder my access to my children and my new partner was prepared to walk away. The children must come first.

During research for this book, other fathers told me in extreme cases you have to be prepared for verbal attacks in the street on both you and your new partner by the ex, by her friends and by her new partner. Others told me their new partners were sent foul-mouthed texts for no reason.

The key is never to respond. See a lawyer and let them do the talking, or if necessary report it to the police. Be prepared for anything and make sure your new partner is well prepared. It will be a test of your love and determination to be a couple.

Showing respect and understanding

It may sound strange but try and be understanding towards your ex-wife during this period, even if she has a new partner or husband. She might be suffering from a psychological problem and need some form of post-divorce counselling.

She may be taking on the role of super-protective mum, but this does not excuse her behaviour. It is often used as an easy excuse by an ex-wife, a 'get out of jail free card' to explain away unacceptable behaviour and harassment. You have to be prepared to say, 'I am prepared to forgive your behaviour. However, in return I would like for us both to work towards moving on with our lives in an appropriate fashion for the good of the children.'

What is sauce for the goose is sauce for gander so it is key you show respect if your ex-wife has a new partner or is on the dating scene.

- If you live in the same town, be respectful of each other's favourite cafés, restaurants and gyms.

- After divorce, friends choose sides, but you may still be invited to the same parties. You need to work out whether one of you should not attend or if you are both happy for you both to go. However, do not back out of an invitation simply to make your ex happy.

- Offer mediation. It may be refused, but you will at least be seen to have tried. It also sets a positive example to your children. Be the bigger person and be businesslike about it.

- If your ex-wife has a new partner you do not know, ask to be introduced; perhaps meet for a coffee or ask your ex for information about him: what he does, whether he has children, whether he is he going through divorce and so on, because these things impact on your children. If you cannot be friends with him, you should at least reach an agreement that you will respect each other's space, position and, most importantly, be friendly and positive in front of the children. Your new girlfriend must also do the same.

● If your ex-wife refuses to meet your new girlfriend, ask her to write a card or letter to your ex, introducing herself. A positive, businesslike gesture like this demonstrates goodwill.

Meeting your children

When introducing a new girlfriend to your children you need to follow these four golden rules:

● You have been out on enough dates by yourselves to feel the relationship has serious possibilities.

● You have been clear with her about what you have been through and your true personal and financial situation.

● You do not introduce a random number of new women to your children; younger children find the concept difficult to cope with and the older children may become defensive.

● Inform your ex-wife.

These four key rules will help make the introduction of a new woman much easier and ensure that you have carefully weighed up her impact on the children's lives and the life of your ex-partner. She must also know she is buying into someone else's emotional baggage, split family and heartache. She has to be a strong woman ready for this sort of commitment.

The way you approach introducing a new girlfriend to your children will vary depending on their ages.

Babies under 18 months

If you have divorced prior to birth or in the first 18 months, your children will never remember mum and dad as a couple. A child under the age of 18 months will not have to be formally introduced.

Simply inform your ex-wife and allow your new partner to interact with the child under your supervision and perhaps that of a friend or relative for short periods of time over a number of weeks or days. The baby will get used to the person.

Always supervise this initial contact and explain the child's routine. Ensure your new partner understands the rules: you supervise, your routine is the rule in your house and while her opinions are welcomed in this sensitive time she will have to appreciate the guidelines and routines negotiated between you and your ex-wife.

Let her learn how you do things with the children and gradually integrate her into their lives. If she has no experience with children, there are courses she can take that will help her learn more about child care and show a level of commitment to you and the children.

Toddlers up to three years old

Children in this age group recognise the people they see regularly in their daily lives. They make associations, which includes recognising mum and dad as a unit. However, children at this age are very flexible and adaptable. The key is to maintain their routine: wake-up times, play schedules, nursery schedule, nights with their mother and nights with their father.

Let your new partner meet the children for an hour first of all and in a group situation: perhaps at a children's party or a family function with relatives. The next meeting should be longer, but, again, in a group situation. The third meeting should be in your home with you, her and the children playing games or perhaps going to the park.

Gradually integrate her into the children's lives. Do not force her on to them, and expect them to be a little sceptical. Think about how the children react when you drop them off at nursery and there is a new carer. They may hide behind you and be tentative, but after a while settle into accepting the new person. Make sure your girlfriend does not try too hard or interfere with the routine. Instead, for successful integration, make her part of the routine and ask her not to try and take over.

You will know the children have accepted her when they start calling her by name or start giving her hugs, holding her hand or wanting her to play with them. Most children will use the same name you use to call her by.

Children from three to ten

The same rules for children between 18 months and three years old apply for this group of children. However, when a child is around six years of age you can start having more grown-up conversations and explain who this person is and why she is important to you. The children are less likely to use tantrums or physical slapping to separate you and will probably more readily articulate their feelings. The key here is to listen to them and understand what they are feeling. If they talk about their mother's reaction to the new girlfriend, you need to address this openly and honestly with them. Always put the children first, but do not let them rule your life.

Your behaviour with your girlfriend

The key rule is: initially, do not hug or cuddle in front of the children. Children of divorce consider their dad to be in their domain; he is theirs, especially when they have their precious time with him. When you do cuddle your girlfriend in front of them for the first time, expect them to reject the concept, become upset or try and stop it. Do not panic; this is all about 'dad ownership'.

Instead, try dancing together and finishing with a group hug involving everyone. Make hugs and handholding a generic group thing. Then, slowly hold your girlfriend's hand. If your youngsters react badly, do not pull away immediately. Instead, invite the child to join in the handholding and explain that you are holding your friend's hand because you like her.

If the child hits the hand clasp or tries to divide the two hands physically, gently let go and let the child become your focal point. Explain that this woman is a special friend and you will be holding her hand sometimes, but it does not mean you love her more than your children. Then revert to group hugs, group dancing, group tickles and handholding.

This behaviour is temporary, and the longer the new partner is in your children's lives the more receptive they will become.

Teenagers

Teenagers are a completely different entity. They can be moody, difficult, badly behaved – and that is prior to divorce! Use the same basic rules as before:

● Talk to teenagers about the concept of a new person in your life and get their feedback. The fact you are doing this ensures they realise you are not forcing a new stepmother on them.

● Ask how they would like to meet the person and how they feel about the concept. Reassure them that their view is important and you will take it into consideration.

● Be prepared for any reaction. Have a plan for a positive and a negative response.

● Discuss a trial period of getting to know the new partner and both promise to meet regularly, say, every week or fortnight, and have a discussion about the new person. Show that you will deal with their concerns in a proactive manner.

● Try to talk to your ex and have her support.

Teenagers will have lots of questions and you are best guided by their response as to how you introduce your new girlfriend. Perhaps they may choose a favourite outing place, the cinema or dinner, but listen carefully to their answers and ask them to respect your desire to move on and find a new partner. Explain you do not want to replace their mother, but that this new person is important to you. It is important that if your children are at the dating age you explain that when they bring their friends home you respect them and you would like the same in return.

The most important thing for the first meeting is to pick a location that everyone is comfortable with and where you can have fun. Do not let your girlfriend try too hard.

Maybe mum and dad will get back together

From the age of three upwards, children are old enough to remember their parents as a family unit. There is sometimes the expectation mum and dad will get back together and children may reject the new partner because of this belief.

The key here is to determine if this is the case by talking to your children. Refer to pages 13–14 and talk over the reasons why you and your wife are no longer together. Explain that no matter what the children do, mum and dad will not be getting remarried, getting back together or living in the same house. Be very, very clear about this.

Agree a trial period during which they agree to be nice to your new friend and get to know her. If possible, talk to your ex and have her provide positive reinforcement that you are not getting back together and that she thinks your new partner is nice.

What if your new partner has children?

Divorce is now so common that it is likely that your new girlfriend is a divorcee and a mother as well. If she has children, they will also need to be introduced to your children. Think carefully about this. You do not want to be introduced to the children, bond with them and then call it all off.

Suggest to your new girlfriend that you meet her children's father to put his mind at ease. The key there is to be businesslike. Assure him that you also have children and have been through divorce, and that you have no intention of replacing him as their father. Stress that you will always be respectful of him and his position in front of the children.

If a meeting is out of the question, try a phone call, letter or e-mail. This can diffuse a situation and is in the best interests of the children and ongoing relationships. The 21st century has brought us a whole range of extended family structures.

Always set the standard and be respectful. But do not let your own children think that your new partner's children will be getting more attention from you than they are.

Introducing your girlfriend's children to yours

If your children are under the age of three, introducing them to your partner's children under supervised conditions should be relatively easy if they are of a similar age.

Introducing your older children to your new partner's younger children may inspire some jealousy. Remember, for example, how your older child behaved when your second one was born. Everyone was concentrating on the new baby and the older child was jealous. So also make a fuss of your child to stop the two-family integration jealousy developing.

Talk to your older children because they may already know the children they are being introduced to, perhaps from school. You may experience jealousy from older children, especially teenagers who feel you are trying to create a new family and push them out. Make extra time to be with and talk to just them and strengthen your relationship.

TOP TIPS FOR INTRODUCING A NEW PARTNER

- Integrating families can be tough, but if it is planned and if you set rules for older children and agree mutual respect, it can work well.
- Initial meetings are best done during group outings to theme parks, the local park or parties and gatherings.
- Do not push the new person on to your children. Take your time; little steps are the best.
- Ensure the children understand that your new girlfriend is not a replacement mum and you are not a replacement dad for your girlfriend's children.
- Act immediately if you see signs of jealousy, aggression or anxiety in any of the children. Consult teachers, counsellors and other family members. Discuss it with your new girlfriend. If the children are old enough, try a group meeting and ask everyone to speak honestly.
- It may take time for acceptance, so be aware about showing affection to your new partner in front of your new partner's children.
- Be patient.

CHAPTER 16

Living and Learning

Great divorced dads have enormous responsibilities and no more so than helping your children through their living and learning phases. No matter how many days a month you have your children, you need to be able to handle anything, especially in the early years. So apart from the topics already covered, what else do you need to know?

Weaning a child from bottle to cups

As a divorced dad you must realise that weaning from bottle to cup will not happen overnight or that your ex will take responsibility for it. She might assume that you are doing it. You also need to realise that you may encounter resistance, tantrums and tears. It is a gradual process.

If your child is bottle fed, you should start introducing a cup with handles and sip-through lid at around 12–18 months old. Start by offering the cup at meals or when they request some juice. Begin with lunch time and then once that is successful use if for the morning feed. Cups with handles improve co-ordination.

As an intermediate stage, use a sports bottle that has a pull-out top and introduce it to your child instead of bottle and teat. This will be the worst when it comes to tantrums and refusals but you must work at it. Remind the child that it is baby behaviour to use a bottle and reward them for using the sports bottle.

If your child has started nursery, they will be watching other children use cups and drinking mugs, so will soon want to use them regularly.

The last bottle to go is what I call the comfort bottle, the night bottle, which toddlers hang on to tenaciously as it helps them get off to sleep and comforts them. Never send your child to bed with juice or cordial. The sugar in it will cause havoc with their baby teeth.

Make sure that you and your ex use the same strategy, otherwise the children will become confused. Talk to her and if possible buy the same drink bottles for night-time milk and the same cups. Consistency and routine that plays out between both homes is essential.

By around age four, your children should be drinking from a cup with no lid. Yes, there will be spillages, but be prepared with the paper towels.

Training your child to feed themselves

Children learn by observation and copying others, so eat with your children and set a good example.

Children from around the age of one are often quite determined to feed themselves and will use their fingers. Let them experience this, but as they get older, cut up small pieces of fruit, cheese, cooked vegetables and other favourite foods so they can pick them up and swallow them easily without choking. Always offer a spoon. They may make a lot of noise with it, but will start experimenting and watching you. Ensure you have plastic bowls and plates and soft plastic cutlery and spoons during the early stages.

A report in 2006 in a national newspaper in Britain revealed that some schools were employing teachers just to show children aged between four and eleven how to use knives and forks. The children knew what they were, but the parents had never taken the time to make sure the child learnt to use them properly. Do not fall into that category.

From around the age of three, talk to your child about how a dinner table is set up and show them the fork, knife and spoon. Demonstrate how to use them and ask them to copy you. Have special cutlery for them so they feel special. At each meal encourage the child to stop using fingers and use their fork and spoon to start with. Children tend to pick up spoon usage if the food is something like baked beans, soup, mashed vegetables, jelly and custard, so think about that when preparing their meal.

When you feel ready to progress, introduce a safe knife and let them get used to it by practising cutting softly cooked carrot batons, for example, so they can enjoy success. Then help them use the knife and fork together. You might need to do this over and over again – dexterity differs from child to child – but reward is important.

Graduate to mini-sized proper cutlery around the age of four. This will make cutting and using a fork easier.

Start bringing the various meal items to the table in different bowls and encourage the children to serve themselves their own portions, another critical element of eating.

It is important that you keep up the encouragement. Ensure they never leave the table without putting their cutlery on the plate, saying thank you and asking to be excused.

Do not eat in front of the TV or at the table with the TV on and do not have toys at the table. This will slow down your child's eating progress, remove their focus and discourage them from using their cutlery. Ensure your children have your full attention and chat to them about what they did that day.

Child-friendly recipes

Following on from the information on pages 97–119, here are some simple recipes to encourage healthy eating.

Breakfast
Prune, blueberry or banana muffins
100 g/7 oz plain (all-purpose) flour
15 ml/1 tbsp sugar
15 ml/1 tbsp baking powder
2.5 ml/½ tsp salt
Cinnamon to taste
1 egg
15 ml/1 oz oil
Either 2 jars of baby food, or 100 g/4 oz puréed prunes, or 3 mashed bananas, or 175 g/6 oz blueberries
15 ml/1 tbsp milk
30 g/2 oz wheat germ

1. Preheat oven to 400°F/200°C/gas 6.

2. Sift the flour, sugar, baking powder, salt, cinnamon and wheat germ into a bowl and make a well in the centre.

3. Place egg, oil, baby food or your choice of fruit and the milk in a medium bowl and beat with a fork until well mixed. Add the wheat germ.

4. Pour the liquid mixture into the flour well and mix just until moistened. The batter will be lumpy.

5. Spoon the mixture into greased muffin tins until they are ¾ full.

6. Bake for 15-20 minutes for regular muffins or 7-9 minutes for mini muffins.

Makes 12 medium muffins or 36 mini muffins.

Lunch and dinner recipes

Dad made it risotto

175 g/6 oz thinly chopped chicken pieces
15 ml/1 tbsp butter
4 rashers of bacon, chopped
1 vegetable stock cube
200 ml/4 oz boiling water
1 carrot, grated
30 ml/2 tbsp broccoli heads, finely chopped
Half a courgette, grated
75 g/3 oz mashed peas
150 g/6 oz easy-cook rice
30 ml/2 tbsp grated cheese

1. Brown the chicken in the butter, together with the bacon.

2. Add the rice and vegetables.

3. Dissolve the stock in the boiling water and add to the pan with the other ingredients.

4. Bring back to the boil, then cover with a lid and cook on a low heat for about 30–40 minutes, until all the stock is absorbed and the rice is cooked. You might need to add more water, so check regularly.

5. Stir in the grated cheese before serving.

Note: you can add any type of meat or remove meat for vegetarians.

Toddler curry

1 onion, chopped
Oil for frying
1 carrot, grated (or chopped, if your children like carrot)
30 ml/2 tbsp broccoli heads, finely chopped
Half a courgette, grated or chopped
75 g/3 oz peas
30 ml/2 tbsp water
175 g/6 oz cooked chicken, chopped
1 jar of mild korma or curry sauce

1. Heat the oil in a pan and sauté the onion.

2. Add in chicken and cook until brown all over.

3. Add the vegetables and water. Bring to the boil then lower the heat and cook gently until the vegetables are tender.

4. Add in curry sauce – ensure it is mild – and heat according to the packet directions.

5. Serve with plain boiled rice.

Note: if the curry is too hot, mix in some yoghurt or coconut milk to cool it down.

Children's fish pie

300 g/12 oz potatoes, peeled and diced
20 ml/1 tbsp + 1 tsp milk
25 g/1 oz butter
Quarter of an onion, finely chopped
1 ripe tomato, skinned, de-seeded and chopped
15 ml/1 tbsp plain (all-purpose) flour
125 g/5 oz cod fillet, skinned and cubed
125 g/5 oz salmon fillet, skinned and cubed
5 ml/1 tsp chopped fresh parsley
100 ml/3½ oz milk
Salt and pepper
30 ml/2 tbsp grated cheese

1. Bring a pan of lightly salted water to the boil, add the potatoes, reduce to a simmer and cook until tender (about 20 minutes). Drain the potatoes and mash with the milk until smooth and season to taste. Keep hot while you make the pie filling.

2. Melt the butter in a saucepan, then add the onion and tomato and sauté until softened.

3. Add the flour and cook for 30 seconds, stirring.

4. Add both sorts of fish to the onion and tomato, together with the parsley.

5. Stir in the milk and season to taste. Simmer for about four minutes until the fish is cooked through.

6. Stir in half of the cheese until melted.

7. Put mixture into a heatproof service dish then top with the mashed potato. Sprinkle the rest of the cheese on top then put under a medium grill until cheese is melted.

Note: You can decorate the top of the pie with two peas to make eyes, some grated carrot to make hair and some more carrot or other vegetables to make a nose and mouth.

Dad's tuna bake
225 g/8 oz shell or corkscrew pasta
30 ml/1 oz butter
15 ml/1 tbsp plain (all-purpose) flour
Salt and pepper
200 ml/7 oz milk
15 ml/1 tbsp grated cheese
30 ml/2 tbsp finely chopped broccoli
30 ml/2 tbsp grated carrot
30 ml/2 tbsp sweetcorn kernels
175 g/6 oz canned tuna, drained

1. Preheat oven to 400°F/200°C/gas 5. In large pan, cook the pasta in lightly salted boiling water.

2. Meanwhile, melt the butter in a pan over low heat. Stir in flour, salt and pepper until blended, then cook for 1 minute, stirring continually.

3. Gradually stir in the milk. Increase the heat to medium and cook, stirring, until the mixture boils and thickens. Boil for 1 minute, stirring frequently.

4. Remove the pan from the heat and stir in half of the cheese until blended.

5. Add the cheese sauce to the pasta and mix together with the vegetables and the tuna. Transfer to a shallow ovenproof dish. Sprinkle with more cheese and bake for 20 minutes.

My dad's stir-fry
Oil for frying
175 g/6 oz chicken, pork or beef, chopped
Half an onion, chopped
1 carrot, chopped
Two broccoli florets, cooked and chopped
30 ml/2 tbsp sweetcorn or peas
45 ml/3 tbsp Chinese greens, chopped
45 ml/3 tbsp mushrooms, chopped
1 packet easy-cook Chinese noodles, cooked
Chicken or vegetable stock
Soy sauce

1. Heat a little oil in a wok or tall-sided pan. Add the meat and stir fry until cooked.

2. Stir in the cooked vegetables and mix thoroughly.

3. Add the noodles and a dash of soy sauce to taste. At this stage, add a little stock if the mixture looks too dry.

4. Stir the mixture thoroughly and ensure that all the ingredients are piping hot before serving.

Note: You will know which vegetables your children prefer. Start with just the meat, Chinese noodles and one vegetable, then add a new vegetable each time you make this dish.

Dad's homemade super spag bol

Oil for cooking
Half an onion, chopped
1 garlic clove, crushed
175 g/6 oz lean minced (ground) beef
75 g/3 oz cooked carrots
50 g/2 oz cooked mushrooms
75 g/3 oz cooked courgette
75 g/3 oz cooked broccoli
1 can of chopped tomatoes
30 ml/2 tbsp tomato paste
Cooked spaghetti

1. Heat the oil over a low heat and gently cook the onion and garlic. Add the meat and brown it all over.

2. Place the cooked vegetables, can of tomatoes and tomato paste in a blender and process until completely smooth.

3. Add the blended mixture to the mince and continue to cook until the meat is cooked through and the sauce is hot.

4. Serve over cooked spaghetti.

Note: The more vegetables you can add to the sauce, the better. For very young children, chop the spaghetti into small pieces that can be spooned; older children like long pieces that they can suck up. See page 112 for more about sneaking vegetables into children's food.

Easy children's pizza

Sauce from Dad's homemade super spag bol recipe (see page 215)
Ready-made pizza base
Chopped cooked ham or other cooked meat
Mixture of chopped vegetables that your children like
Grated cheese

1. Spread the sauce on to the pizza base.

2. Allow your children to top the pizza with a selection of their favourite cooked meats and vegetables. Sprinkle grated cheese over the top.

3. Cook under a medium grill until the cheese is melted.

Note: There are no quantities given in this recipe because pizza topping is a matter of personal taste. You can also use pita bread instead of a pizza base.

Family shepherd's pie

Oil for cooking
Half an onion, chopped
350 g/12 oz lean minced (ground) meat
200 ml/7 oz sauce from Dad's homemade super spag bol (see page 215)
350 g/12 oz potatoes, boiled and mashed
75 g/3 oz butter
100 g/4 oz grated cheese

1. Preheat an oven to 375°F/190°C/gas 5.

2. Heat the oil in a pan and gently cook the onion until soft.

3. Add the meat and cook until browned all over. Stir in the sauce and bring to the boil stirring occasionally, then transfer to an ovenproof dish.

4. Stir half the cheese into the mashed potatoes and place on top of the meat and sauce mixture.

5. Sprinkle the rest of the cheese on top of the potatoes.

6. Cook for about 15 minutes until the top is golden brown.

Note: Some children will eat chunky vegetables in this pie.

Dad's homemade burgers

350 g/12 oz lean minced (ground) meat
1 egg, beaten
50 g/2 oz breadcrumbs
Half an onion, finely chopped
Olive oil
15 ml/1 tbsp plain (all-purpose) flour
Burger buns, preferably wholemeal
Sliced tomato, cooked bacon and grated cheese, to finish

1. Mix together the mince, egg, breadcrumbs and onion. If mixture is a little dry, add a little olive oil, but do not make it sticky.
2. Take a small handful of the mixture. Roll into a ball, then roll the ball in flour. Place on to a greased baking tray and then push ball down to flatten it into a burger shape.
3. Cook under a medium grill for about three minutes each side or until the burgers are thoroughly cooked.
4. Place the cooked burgers, buns, tomato, bacon and cheese on separate serving plates and allow children to build their own burgers.

Dad's tacos

350 g/12 oz lean minced (ground) meat or vegetarian alternative
Oil for frying
½ can red beans or baked beans
175 ml/6 oz sauce from Dad's homemade super spag bol (see page 215)
Ready-made mild taco seasoning
Grated cheese
Sweetcorn
Chopped lettuce
Very mild chilli sauce
Taco shells
Sour cream

1. Cook the meat in a little oil and brown all over.
2. Add the beans and sauce, together with taco seasoning to taste. This can be quite spicy so be careful with younger children. Continue to cook, stirring occasionally, until the sauce is hot and the meat is thoroughly cooked.
3. Warm the taco shells according to the directions on the packet.
4. Lay out other items in separate dishes
5. Serve the cooked meat sauce and all the other items separate and allow the children to create their own tacos.

Potty training

Potty training is something that cannot be avoided. Even if you only see your children for one day a week, you still have to understand the basics of potty training and how to handle all the eventualities. There is no sugar coating it: potty training is messy and smelly; but as a committed dad you should never shy away from it. It is part of life and your children need you to help them learn.

Toddlers can be ready to start potty training anywhere from 18 to 24 months. Signs that they might be ready include:

- Starting to show an interest in the toilet.

- Having a regular bowel movement at the same time each day.

- Urinating about 20–30 minutes after a big drink.

- Staying dry for at least two hours during the day and being dry after short sleeps during the day.

- Playing with or sitting on the potty you have bought.

- Saying they do not like nappies and want to wear knickers.

- Saying nappies are for babies.

- Becoming visibly upset or embarrassed when they have wet or soiled their nappy.

- You start to notice little actions they do before they do a wee or poo. I call this the Wee-wee Dance!

If you have noticed three or more of these signs, talk to your child's mother about her observations and agree a plan. If your child is at nursery, talk to the carers because they might be able to confirm that it is time and offer you advice.

Then you need to buy:

- Potty – preferably more than one.

- Children's toilet seat – this fits over your ordinary seat and makes children feel safe and ensures they do not fall in.

- Pull-up nappies.

- Children's hand wash.

- Toilet training wipes – they are gentle on your child's skin.

- Story book on potty training.

- Stickers and reward gifts with a potty training chart.

- Knickers and pull-up nappy pants – lots, at least 10.

- Children's step × 2 – one for reaching the toilet and one for reaching the basin.

- Clean-up kit for messes.

Key potty training steps

You will need to explain to your child what you expect of them and show them. Your child must be able to tell you he has to go or you must notice the Wee-wee Dance and immediately take them to the toilet. Undress them and pop them on the potty, and encourage them to use it. In the early stages, you might find yourself doing this every half-hour or so. Finish by wiping, dressing and hand washing. Keep rewarding in a positive and consistent way.

You should begin by taking your child into the toilet with you and talk about what you are doing. For dads, it is easier to show little boys how to go to the toilet. However, boys normally start potty training sitting down, primarily due to balance issues, and gradually learn to stand

With girls, ensure their mother has taken them to the toilet with her. Alternatively, you can explain that boys and girls are different, and that girls sit down to use the toilet. You can pretend to be a girl and sit down and show her the movements. Remember that girls wipe front to back.

Make sure you choose a specific word to refer to what a child is doing, e.g. wee or pee, or poo or poop. Do not change the words and do not use rude words. Ensure the same language is used at their mother's house, as well as by their nursery carers and babysitters, if you use them.

You should introduce the potty to the child, allow them to see it and play with it. Also show them the children's toilet seat and step, and show them how to use them.

When you go to the toilet, put the potty down and encourage your child to sit on it. Have some toys nearby so they can play, as it might take a while. After you have used the toilet, put the children's toilet seat on and let them try using the step. Some children do have a fear of sitting on the toilet, so use the child seat and hold them on, assuring them they are safe. Others hate the flush sound, so flush with them and tell them it is actually a friendly dragon or other fish or whale saying hello or that you are watering the plants.

Put your child on the potty at the same time every morning and encourage a wee or a poo when you know they normally do. Then every 20 minutes or so, ask if they want to do a wee-wee and encourage them to tell you.

The first wee or poo in the potty will be a big event, so heap praise on the child and consistently offer a reward. I suggest doing up a chart with the child's name, a picture of them from an old photo, and squares. Using their favourite stickers, every time they use the potty they get a sticker and then when the chart is complete they get a bigger present. Make sure this present is wrapped and ready before you start the training, so they know it exists. Do not get angry if they mess themselves in the early stages. Make sure you have potties in the bedroom, living room and bathroom, as bladder control is still limited.

Put potty training pull-up nappies on them first and make a big thing about how grown-up this is. Practise pulling them up and down; make a game of it. Remember, though, you are going to go through a lot each day.

After a number of successful wees, move on to knickers for half a day and pull-ups for the other half, then a week later progress to knickers only. You will find your child will start refusing to wear nappies altogether and this is a sign they are progressing well and you are doing a good job. Even when you go out, keep asking every 20 minutes and maybe keep a spare potty in the car for emergencies, together with knickers, wipes and nappies.

When your child has learned to use the toilet consistently during the day, you may be able to take the nappy off at night. Your child may be ready to begin when the nappy stays dry more and more often overnight. Try half waking the child late in the evening and take them to the toilet. When they are half asleep they are likely to do a wee and go straight back to sleep. Limit the child's fluid intake just before bedtime as this will help with bladder control and hopefully lead to a dry night. Again, use rewards for a dry night.

Never criticise – always encourage. This means you have to remain calm because it will get frustrating and appear to dominate your life. There are books you can get to read at bedtime that tell stories about a little girl or boy learning to potty train.

Potty training problems

Sometimes your child will have been doing very well and then all of a sudden you get reports from nursery they are wetting themselves or they do it when they are with you. This can be caused by:

- Being given too many fluids before their nursery drop-off. Make sure you and your ex agree to limit fluid intake before the drop-off.

- The child being overtired or unwell.

- Negative experiences at your ex-wife's house. Talk to her to find out if this is the case.

- Attention seeking.

- Fear of flushing or sitting on the toilet – offer reassurance and rewards to overcome this.

- Physical problems. Some children develop a urinary tract infection (sometimes due to strong detergents such as bubble bath) that causes pain during urination. Boys might have a blockage of the penile opening. Some children have a very small bladder, or dietary problems causing discomfort. Be sure to see your doctor if you suspect any possibility of physical reasons for regression.

The best way I found to reverse potty training regression was a mixture of reward and positive reinforcement.

I made a large picture of a castle with my son and daughters' photographs at the top of castle. Leading up to the castle, I painted a pathway of stones and every day they had a dry day they got a sticker. At the castle were gates that opened and showed a picture of a present. I had the presents wrapped and sitting next to the castle so they could see them. They were told when they got their sticker path filled up they would receive the present. It worked well, and while there were still a few wet days, the focus was on the present.

With my daughter I told her she could not wear her pretty dress if she wet herself, but would have to wear trousers. It worked for her, because she loves dresses and dislikes trousers.

Bedwetting

Once a child is potty trained, your next concern will be bed wetting, or nocturnal enuresis to give it its technical name. It is very common, and can affect children even into their teens.

After your child has learned to stay dry during the day, you can start encouraging night time dryness. Bladder size and muscle strength are required before a child is physically able to remain dry throughout the night, so for some children, their bodies may not yet be mature enough to stay dry. For others, simple encouragement like talking and offering incentives for dry nights helps motivate a child. With bedwetting there is often a physical component as well, such as slow bladder growth, sound sleeping, physical abnormalities or a hormone deficiency.

Bedwetting key rules

- More important than wet sheets is your child's self esteem. As children get older, they will become more aware that this is not the norm and may feel ashamed.

- Stay positive about it and let the child know it is not their fault; their body is just not ready yet.

- Consult your doctor about possible physical problems, especially if the child is between six and thirteen years of age.

- Reduce drinks before bed.

- Put your child on the toilet a couple of hours after they go to bed. Most youngsters will wee in their sleep and can be put back to bed without drama.

- Keep bedwetting discussions private with older children; stop any teasing straight away from brothers and sisters. You need to tell them the problem will go away and talk to them about any possible worries they have at school or their other house.

- Make sure they have access to a supply of clean sheets and plastic under sheets so they can learn to strip their beds themselves.

Some medical problems can cause bedwetting, including bladder infections, some allergies, diabetes, constipation and stress.

Teaching children to dress and undress themselves

A critical element of living and learning is helping your child develop independence. Learning to undress and dress themselves is an important element of that and makes children feel very grown up.

Your children will learn to undress themselves before dressing themselves. It comes with the territory: they learn to pull down their pants for potty training and to take off outdoor coats. Here are some helpful pointers:

- Buy clothes that are easy to pull off, with generous necks, and trousers and skirts with elasticated waistbands. Try to avoid buttons and zips.

- Encourage your children to undress themselves and provide praise each time they achieve success or move on to a different, harder piece of clothing.

- Use a chart with pictures of tops, skirts, dresses and knickers and give a sticker when your child manages to take them off.

- As part of the process, show them the laundry bin for dirty clothes. Start good habits early.

- For buttons, zips and shoelaces, break the process down so that, for instance, they do one button and you do the rest. Children learn to zip up and down before learning to put the zip together. Practise with them and offer rewards for success.

- Nursery schools work hard at encouraging children to learn to put on their own shoes after soft room play or to take off fleeces when they feel hot, so keep in touch with carers.

- At school nursery and reception class, your child will require a PE kit and the first term is spent teaching the children how to put on their shorts and t-shirts and take off their main uniform. Don't be surprised if you collect your child on PE afternoon to discover their main school uniform on back to front with trousers on the wrong way. Praise them for the achievement.

Once children come to terms with undressing they move to another independent stage, dressing, and that normally means they want to pick out their own clothes to wear. Let them do it. It might mean a mismatch of colours and outfits, but it is their choice and their success. They may struggle to get the clothes on, but do not step in unless you hear cries of frustration.

You can try laying out clothes to choose from, but do not offer young children too many choices or it will frustrate and confuse them and you will end up with tears. Two options are the best.

Use a dressing chart and focus on the harder things like buttons and laces once your child has mastered the basics. Beware the lazy child. Some children just do not want to bother, so ensure the TV is off, get them excited about doing a grown-up task, and use a reward chart. Even if they just manage their knickers, it is still an achievement! Once they can put on their knickers and vests, move them on to tops and trousers or skirts and dresses. Be around to help if needed, but offer only limited assistance. Do not leave the room as the child will just give up and think they have had a victory. Be strong and encouraging.

Observation, help, encouragement, reward and a step-by-step approach in line with the nursery and school will work.

Teaching your children good manners

This comes directly from the way you behave. If you are rude and bad mannered and yell at people, never say please and thank you, and ignore questions, your child will follow suit. So if that is you, clean up your act now, and the same goes for your ex-wife. This is another occasion when adopting a businesslike approach with your ex is critical; by being polite and well mannered towards her, despite the hurt you feel, you set a good example to your children.

Children require positive role models for manners and a great divorced dad:

● Constantly uses please and thank you.

● Never argues with adults or the children's mother in front of the children.

● Is never rude to other adults in front of the children, especially to their mother.

● Never walks out of rooms or fights in front of the children with their mother or a relative.

The key step is to keep calm at all times and start with the basics:

● Never give your child an item unless they say please. I refer to it as 'the magic word'.

● Insist on a thank you; otherwise the item is removed.

● Ensure your children apologise to each other or you if their misbehaviour affects others.

● Insist on them saying hello and goodbye by setting the example. Making a game of it: 'See you later, alligator' is a fun way for toddlers to get used to saying goodbye.

● Use the naughty step to punish bad manners.

Remember: set the example, constantly remind the child and reward positive behaviour. For more advice on table manners, see page 103.

If older children who have had perfect manners suddenly start misbehaving, then you need to get to the bottom of it. It is critical to act quickly and use discipline, such as reducing time on the computer or games console or introducing a curfew.

If possible, discuss this problem with your ex-wife, because no matter how much pain you have been through, you have a joint responsibility to notice changes and act on them. Brattish behaviour may be a way of rebelling, but there comes a point when it should stop. See page 91 for more on teenager misbehaviour.

Training your child to go to bed on time

As we have discussed in our chapter on children and health, a child that's had a good night's sleep and sufficient naps is a healthy and happy child (see page 158).

Key to this is routine. No matter what age, children need routine around bedtime, so draw up a chart like the one below, which sets out an afternoon routine for school terms.

Toddlers	Age 4–6	Age 6–11	Teenagers
If collected at 5 pm, take home, unpack bags, admire craft items.	3 pm Collect from school, unpack bags at home, snack of fruit, cheese or cracker, admire school work and hang it up.	3 pm Collect from school. Child may attend after-school sports practice, ballet, singing, piano or other lessons. When they get home, offer a healthy snack (no sugary drinks). Help them with their homework.	Walk, ride or bus home from school or after-school activity. Set a strict deadline for when they need to be home and when they should start homework.
5.15–5.30pm Free play.	3.30–5pm Free play. Discourage TV, encourage toys and helping to prepare dinner.	5–7pm Can include limited TV or computer time as agreed with you. Encourage children to help prepare dinner.	6–7pm Should include assistance with dinner preparation and time for you to chat with your teen.

Toddlers	Age 4–6	Age 6–11	Teenagers
5.30 pm Dinner.	5 pm Dinner.	7 pm Dinner.	7 pm Dinner.
6 pm Bath time. Then PJs on, read book from nursery bag and other books.	5.30pm Bath time Then PJs on, allow some quietening down play in bedroom. Read books from school bag and make notes in child's teacher reading book, read some more books.	7.30 pm Dinner.	7.30–8pm Dependent on the teen. Some have morning showers, but ensure daily cleanliness.
7pm Lights out.	7–7.30pm Lights out.	8 pm Quietening down and bed preparation. Try to encourage reading. Then lights out at 8.30pm.	8 pm onwards More homework and negotiated computer/games console time and curfew. Lights out between 9 and 10 pm to ensure your teen is rested. Keep TVs and computers out of the bedroom if possible and ensure the children do not stay up texting friends on mobile phones.

Children aged between two and four often need day time naps, which can last between 30 minutes and three hours. Signs that naps are needed include grizzling, misbehaving and fighting with other children, falling asleep while playing and not sharing toys.

Getting a child to sleep

The sooner you start your new sleep routine and stick to it, the better, especially with toddlers. Young children will fight sleep, so it is up to you to provide routine and discipline to get them to bed on time.

Sleep training is popular and involves using the routine as laid out for toddlers on page 226 and then putting them down in their bed, sitting with them for a few minutes of cuddles, then saying goodnight and leaving the room. Ensure there is a nightlight and you have black out blinds for summer nights. The child is then likely to try refusing to go to sleep and will cry. You have to be strong. Let them cry for up to ten minutes and you are likely to find they will settle themselves.

If not, check to make sure there is nothing seriously wrong. Then give your child a cuddle and kiss and walk away, closing the door. It can be painful, but once the toddler realises you will not give the attention they are after, they will fall asleep.

The same process applies to a child between three and five years old. However, more interaction in terms of book reading and a defined quietening down time is critical. Be strict about lights out and ensure they know the rules, particularly with children moving between homes.

There will be tears and that would have been tough enough when you had your wife to share it with; but now you are divorced, you might feel extra guilty that your child will hate you because you adhere to a routine. They won't; children test their barriers and it is your responsibility to ensure they get a healthy sleep to remain happy and content.

As the children grow older you must maintain routine, but show some flexibility. Check they have not taken in mobile phones, games consoles or other computer games to play after lights out. Use your discipline lists for failing to adhere to the routine or breaching curfews.

Sleep problems

Your children may encounter sleep problems and it is important that you tackle this, because you do not want crabby children or to take tired children to their mother. Try to discuss sleep problems with your ex.

Many households have children sharing rooms and often you will have a good sleeper and bad sleeper. Move the good sleeper out for a week, perhaps to a cot in your room or a spare room or living room, and sleep train the bad sleeper.

Some children wake in the middle of the night and try to climb into your bed. It is important to comfort the child and allow them to fall asleep in your bed and then take them straight back to their own bed. There are no hard and fast rules about letting children over the age of two sleep with their mother or father. Find what is comfortable for you, but do not let the children take over the bed all the time, as you need space too. They might be seeking comfort or simply a cuddle from a bad dream so be gentle. However, do not let it become a habit.

If your child is scared of the dark, try using a night light. They can also take comfort from a favourite blanket or teddy bear.

Make sure the older children in the house are aware of the younger children's sleep routines and encourage good, quiet behaviour before bedtime.

Children and pocket money

As a divorced dad, you will find yourself worrying about money, often because you may have maintenance payments to make, as well as meeting your own costs. So, as you economise, use this opportunity to teach your children the value of money.

Children as young as three to five can be taught about money:

● Take them to the supermarket and let them hand over the money and accept change.

● At the DVD rental shop, let your children pick out the film they want and give them the money to hand over to pay for it.

● Take them out shopping once a week perhaps to a pound shop and give them a pound and show them the area they can choose something from.

● You can buy paint-your-own piggy-banks from toy stores. Buy one and paint it with your child. Then every time they are given money, even if it is a penny, put it in the piggy-bank.

Children from six to eleven years of age are likely to be given pocket money. The amount varies from family to family, whether divorced or not. This is another topic that you and your ex will have to discuss. It should not be up to one parent to pay the entire pocket money. Each should contribute some, so decide on a total amount and how it will be shared between you. Otherwise you will end up with two problems:

● Children coining it by getting double pocket money – an amount from each house.

● Your ex-wife is likely to say, 'Ask your father' (or vice versa, of course), and you will end up spending more money on top of maintenance payments.

The key is be fair. Talk to other parents at the school and find out what they give their children as pocket money.

Set rules for earning pocket money. For example, your child must complete a list of chores at your house and/or their mum's and keep their room(s) clean. If you use a chart you will see when some of these chores have not been done, and that means less pocket money. Negotiate pocket money rises or extras on each birthday.

Encourage your child into the saving habit by putting a small amount of the pocket money into a piggy-bank or bank account each week, even if it is just a few coins.

If you want to make sure your child spends productively you can get special gift cards from stores such as Woolworths, W H Smith, Boots and other major stores that allow you to put a specific amount on the card that the child can use like a credit card. This is especially good for teenagers (see page 153 for funding books for school and study materials). The card can be topped up with more funds at your discretion.

Teenagers like to buy their own clothes and shoes and often school books, so I would suggest negotiating a normal pocket money rise on each birthday or every six months, as long as your child can justify why the increase is needed. This is important in developing their independent negotiating life skills.

For clothes and shoes, negotiate an allowance each month.

You will also need to tackle the issue of mobile phones. Teenagers should pay for their own mobile phones from their pocket money. If they run out of credit, they will either have to get a part-time job or take an advance on next month's pocket money. Mobile phones are important for children in divorced families because they allow them free access to both parents.

Never give in. By all means give them extra jobs around the house but make them earn the cash.

Teaching your teenagers the value of money and encouraging them to earn extra cash for extra items they want is important. Encourage them to take on a part-time job, but as a great divorced dad you should ensure that:

● Their mother is agreeable.

● The job is suitable.

● It fits around the custody schedule and your teenager's schooling.

● It is not too demanding and does not interfere with a healthy lifestyle.

● They agree to save part of the money they earn.

To do a part-time job, your teen will need approval from both parents, so I suggest a family meeting if the relationship between you all allows it. Try and put anger aside so that your teenagers know that you support the venture and that you and your ex are agreed on the guidelines and rules around the job.

Guide to children's clothing

It is not uncommon after a divorce for the wife to take most of the children's clothing with her, which can make life difficult for the divorced dad. Instead, try to share the clothes in a reasonably equal way before the actual split, so each new household has something of everything, including familiar blankets and bedding. It is also only natural that the parent who has the children for the majority of the time takes more clothes, but if you have shared residency you should divide the clothes equally. However, because you are moving on with your children and starting a new life at your house, when they are with you try to put together some new clothes that stay at your house to give the children ownership of them there.

I put together a set of basic clothes for my children that always stays at my house. I based this on my share of their original clothes, but then added to it as necessary. I bought some items from low-cost stores such as Primark, Asda and Tesco and I always took the children with me so they could play a role in the choice of item. Some came as gifts from friends and family. There are good bargains to be had on bundles of clothes from eBay and from charity shops.

The key, however, was sitting down and writing a list of things I knew the children needed. I worked on the theory that they would need a duplicate of the things they had at their mother's home. Part of me also wanted to get new items not associated with my former family home to signify the new start. However, this would have been costly and not given my children the continuity they needed in having familiar clothes and bedding.

Below are my suggested must-have lists for all ages. Your children will tell you what extras they want and need.

Babies 0–18 months

- All-in-one baby grows (4).
- Short sleeve no leg baby-grows (4).
- Trousers (2 pairs) for boy or girl.
- Long sleeve tops (2) for boy or girl.
- Short sleeve tops (2) for boy or girl.
- Tights (2 pairs) for girl baby.
- Winter dresses (2) for girl.
- Summer dresses (2) for girl.
- Overalls for boy or girl.
- Winter fleece (2).
- Winter coat.

- Woollen cap, mittens and gloves.

- Pyjamas (2).

- Sleep suits (2).

- Socks (3 pairs).

- Shoes.

- Raincoat.

- Summer hat.

This list is based on one day and you can multiply this depending on how many days you have them or how often you are willing to do the washing and drying. Bear in mind that young children have accidents and can often go through a number of outfits a day, so the more clothes you can get together the better. When they grow out of them, you can sell them on eBay or swap with friends who have younger children. Children grow quickly during this period, so check size regularly.

Toddlers

- T-shirts (2).

- Skirts (2) for girl.

- Trousers (2) for boy or girl.

- Shorts (2) for boy or girl.

- Long sleeve winter tops (2).

- Fleece.

- Winter coat.

- Rain coat.

- Pyjamas (2), long sleeve for winter, short sleeve for summer.

- Dresses (2) for girl.

- Swimming kit.

- Shoes – one pair that stays with child and goes between parents is fine, but I suggest a back-up pair as well.

- Wellingtons.

- Nursery uniform, one set for summer and one for winter.

- Knickers (5 pairs at least).

This list is also a per-day list – toddlers love mud, getting messy and if you are potty training you'll need a number of outfits, the more spare the better. Make sure your children know where the spare knickers are and if they have nursery bags show them you are putting in spare knickers and a pair of trousers or skirt so they can show the carers.

Little toddler girls love pink. They may go through a phase of wanting to wear only pink, or only skirts and dresses.

Five to nine-year-olds

- School uniform, one set for summer and one for winter.

- Formal school shoes.

- Gym shoes.

- Going-out shoes.

- Wellingtons.

- Raincoat.

- Winter coat.

- Fleece.

- Summer top.

- Winter top.

- Skirt for girls.

- Dress for girls.

- Jeans for boys and girls.

- Trousers for boys.

- Shorts for boys and girls.

- Swimming kit.

- Going-out outfit.

- Pyjamas – one set for summer and one for winter.

- Winter hat, scarf and gloves.

- Summer hat.

- Coat and/or separate raincoat.

This is a basic list designed around one day's wear, depending on the weather and the season. Children this age love being involved in buying their own clothes, so take them shopping, give them a budget and point them in the right direction.

Ensure you and your ex-wife decide formally who pays what for school kit. If you have the children at the weekend and do not collect them directly from school but from their mother's house, make sure that she has provided you with their school uniform, backpacks and homework so you can have them ready for school on Monday without any fuss. It is important to avoid the, 'Oh, I'll drop it around later,' scenario because it interferes with your plans and often the other party may forget. You must set the standard by being organised and returning all clothing items cleaned and washed and all kit. Having said that, I always have a spare school set at my house as a back-up, including school fleeces and coats.

Check the lost property bin at your child's nursery and school regularly.

Teenagers

Teenagers start to make their own choices and peer pressure and fashion become more of an issue, so although their basic clothing needs are similar to younger children, you will find requests for more pairs of jeans, special trainers, trendy jackets, a variety of shoes and boots or sports clothing – skateboard outfits, horse-riding gear, tennis gear, or whatever your teen chooses. These all need to be negotiated according to your income and what you can afford, what your teenager's pocket money can afford, and what you and your ex-wife will allow.

Teenagers tend to wear the same favourite clothes, so they will be likely to bring their clothes with them, rather than keep a set at each house. They are also more likely to go shopping with their friends, rather than you or their mum, so it is important they know what clothes you and your ex-wife will allow. You should also discuss budgets with them. You can either give the children cash or you can open a special account and get a Solo debit card for them. They can then use this card and once they have spent their limit, that's it, or they do extra household chores to earn extra money.

Clothing name tags

Take it from me: iron-on name tags for your children's clothes are critical. At nursery and school, children's clothes can go missing or get mixed up, especially because as part of nursery and reception class they get lessons in changing clothes and have to learn to change for PE. Imagine 20 children in a room and you can see how keeping track of clothes can be tough.

Name tags also help you and your children clearly define which clothes you have purchased and which clothes should be returned to your house after a visit to mum's house. It is a good idea if your ex-wife uses a different coloured or type of name tags, so the children and you can separate out which clothes must go back to their mother's house.

You can also buy sew-on name tags, but who has the time!

Buying clothes

Try to be smart when buying clothes. Seek out good quality basics like underwear, fleeces, school uniforms from chain stores like Tesco, Asda, Woolworths and Marks and Spencer. These stores offer very good and reasonably priced children's ranges that children actually want to wear. Look for clothes in the sales and remember to add extras at each change of season.

There are certain clothes you should not skimp on. Always buy good quality and properly fitted shoes. Your children also deserve a good quality coat. There may be cheap imitations, but you will find the buttons fall off, zips break and they are not as hard wearing as an item of a slightly higher price. Quality school uniforms are important, too, because they will get washed daily.

Bear in mind that your children will want some special clothes, as well. It may be a party dress, special trainers or a specialist t-shirt. Remember that children probably do not care where you buy their underwear, but might be truly hurt if presented with the wrong trainers.

As long as it fits your budget, involve your children and work out what is needed, what is important and what is not, and spend accordingly. However, do not be a pushover and kit them out in designer gear out of guilt.

Clothes fights

Many divorced couples will tell you that missing clothes are a constant form of frustration with one parent claiming the other is deliberately withholding clothes to upset them. Some mums, for example, have been known to keep clothes they know the father purchased because they think he should be paying more maintenance. Some dads may keep clothes they know the mother loves just as a way of punishment. In other words, warring parties believe what cannot be achieved one way is achieved by another. If this is you, stop it! Settle disputes with name tags that clearly distinguish your clothes from your ex's. Remember the financial settlement and monetary deals you made and stick to them. Parents should never try and get the upper hand by having the other pay for extra clothes by default because they think they got a raw deal.

Special clothes to stay at your house

If you buy clothes that you want to remain at your house, or if your children receive them as a gift from, say, your parents, it is important that you are clear they are to stay with you.

Be clear with the children, no matter what their age. Simply say, 'No, this top is special and stays at this house.' For little ones, put the new clothes away before the transfer back to the other house or reassure the child that you will keep it safe for the next visit.

If they really want to show their mum a new outfit, take a photo of them in it that they can show that to their mother. That's the beauty of digital cameras, take a snap and print it off on your printer and let the children take that home. You can even take pictures on some mobile phones. It keeps everyone happy.

However, on handover be clear it was the child's wish to show the mother the picture and that it is not an attempt by you to upset her or show off.

Emergency car clothes kit

A great divorced dad is always prepared, so I strongly recommend you keep a travel kit in your car at all times, just in case. It should contain the following:

- T-shirt.
- Fleece.
- Trousers or skirt.
- Body suit, if there is a baby in the family.
- Knickers.
- Couple of nappies and wipes for younger children.
- Socks or tights.
- Spare pair of old shoes.
- Umbrella.
- Sunhat.
- Towel.
- Blanket.
- Spare pair of trousers, a top and a fleece for you.

This emergency kit will serve you well. You never know when you will need a spare outfit, a towel or a blanket. Keep the kit in a bag in the boot and you will always be ready in an emergency. It is best to use old clothes that are not worn much and can stay in the car as your emergency back up supply. The number of times my emergency kit has been come in handy for myself or friends is immeasurable.

Clothes washing

The old-fashioned idea that the woman does the washing is rubbish! To be a great divorced dad, you'll need a washing machine and a dryer – and it'll take only minutes to work out that they are dead easy to use. Here are some basic tips:

- Separate coloured and whites. Brightly coloured children's clothes do have a habit of running, very badly.

- I find a biological liquid detergent best, preferably a good quality one with fabric softener in it. You can get fabric softener separately, but it is just another thing to remember.

- Biological detergents get clothes cleaner, but can cause irritation in some children so switch to a non-bio or organic detergent such as that made by Ecover.

- You can buy scented sheets to throw in a tumble dryer. These make the clothes smell nicer, more homely and reduce ironing.

- Clean the lint filter on the dryer regularly.

- Wash daily when the children are with you as dirty clothes, especially when toilet training, will smell and you need to get them clean fast. Ensure older children help with the washing and make teenagers responsible for doing a load for themselves.

- If you have toddlers, check their nursery bags because if they have had accidents at nursery the wet items will be in plastic bags for you to wash.

- When my children were toddlers they loved to help sort the dried clothes. Making dad's pile, mum's pile, and a pile for themselves and so forth was great fun and we made a game of these things.

- Young children also have a fascination loading the washing machine so supervise your toddler and let them learn about helping you out. However, be warned: toddlers have a habit of pushing buttons, which stop the machines mid-cycle, so fit a safety cover over the buttons.

Talking to your children about sex

Children are becoming sexually aware younger and younger, so it is important that you as a dad are comfortable discussing sex. Agree a plan with your ex, perhaps she will talk to your daughter about sex and periods, while you will talk to your son. Whoever does the talking, you must agree on what is to be said.

Sex education varies from school to school, so find out what the policy is at your children's as it might cover issues your child will have questions about.

Be aware that children have access to the internet and phone lines, and that sex is openly shown in movies and it is all around them. There are various ways to approach the issue. The best way is openly and honestly. Talk to them about sex. There are plenty of books available that give advice on this. Always answer questions truthfully and without embarrassment. The Family Planning Association can be a good initial source of material and advice.

When your teen starts dating seriously, it is up to you to set rules about sex and contraception. Again, this is a discussion that needs to involve your ex. You need to be aware that no matter how good an upbringing a child has, if they want to have sex they will, so talking to them about contraception to protect against aids, STDs and pregnancy is vital. Set rules for what goes on in your home, but also be aware that sex happens anywhere. You may have to revisit the topic of sex and body changes a number of times. With good advice your children should make the right choices and be safe and healthy.

Teaching your child about bullying

As a divorced dad, you should be prepared to recognise signs that your child is being bullied and help them deal with it. Do not forget during the pre-divorce period they might have witnessed their parents trying to bully each other and that may make them more susceptible. You have to confront this issue and ensure your child can stand up for their rights and will not be victimised.

Warning signs of bullying include:

● Sudden low self esteem and an obvious decline in friends.

● Not wanting to go to school, taking an unusual route or insisting you drive them.

● Belongings go missing, school uniforms are torn or there are unexplained bruises or injuries.

● Mood swings.

- Interrupted sleep and bad dreams.
- Eating less.
- Not wanting to take part in school events and sports.
- Regular complaints of illness to get out of school.
- Decline in grades.

A great divorced dad takes immediate action.

- Discuss with your ex-wife, if possible, to ask if she has noticed similar symptoms.
- Talk to your child and make it clear you will not tolerate bullying. They will probably deny it for fear of retribution, but you must protect their self-esteem and explain that by not standing up to bullies it gives them the power.
- Talk to your child about why they are being bullied: is it because of the divorce, because they are small in size or good at school? By identifying the reason for the bullying you can move forward more productively. This might take time and it might be embarrassing for your child to admit the real reason, but once the reason is identified you are halfway there.
- Talk to the child's teacher and ask for advice and the school's bullying policy. Make it clear you want the bullying to stop and will assist in any way possible.
- Spend extra time with your child, especially at school events, and try to rebuild their confidence.
- Talk to them about a non-violent, non-abusive method for dealing with bullies.
- Encourage them to have friends over to your house in their own environment to rebuild confidence.
- If necessary, seek help from a school counsellor or external counsellors. They will be able to offer possible alternative ways of dealing with the bullying. Talking to a third party will boost your confidence and that of your child.

The most important thing is to give your child the skills and confidence to tackle the bullying themselves in a non-violent but effective manner.

Teens and drugs

We have all heard the horror stories of drugs being sold at school gates and parents suddenly discovering the child they thought was an angel is using some form of illegal substance. At school, children are taught about the dangers of drugs and not to use them, so as a great divorced dad you must find out from the teachers what your children have been taught and how. You should then reinforce it at home. I strongly recommend you should have a drug talk with your child as well, like you did for sex education.

Warning signs that your child is using drugs include:

- Missing cash.

- Odd behaviour and mood swings.

- Dramatic alteration to sleeping patterns, such as not getting up until midday and staying out all night.

- Refusal to stick to routine.

- Sudden disappearances.

- Lethargic behaviour.

If you witness any of the above symptoms, don't panic.

- Talk to your ex to see if she has noticed the same symptom.

- Talk to your child and discuss your suspicions. Ask them to explain their behaviour changes.

- Reinforce the dangers of drug use.

- Encourage them to see their doctor, with or without you.

If they deny it, you can buy drug swab kits on the internet, so you could challenge your child to regular tests or ask them to prove you wrong by having the family doctor do it.

If you discover drug use, seek immediate, confidential support and advice from either your GP or a drugs helpline. For a long-term problem, you might have to consider rehab or a family intervention.

How to keep your family communicating

It is important that your children realise that everyone, including them, has a voice, so organise regular family meetings and find out what issues need discussing.

As a great divorced dad, make time every day your child is with you just to sit and chat, even if it is only for ten minutes. It is important that they know you care and will listen. Yes, as they grow up your children will go through the talking stage, the non-talking stage and so forth, but you need to understand that this is a mix of hormones and children being children. Just watch out for warning signs that could show you your child is depressed due to the divorce or having problems they are embarrassed to talk to you about. These signs include:

- Non-communication.

- Misbehaviour.

- Bad language.

- Young children may suddenly start wetting the bed or not using the toilet after they are toilet trained.

- Dressing unusually.

- Sleeping a lot.

- Not sleeping at all.

- Tantrums.

- Not sticking to rules.

- Problems at school.

- Being overly clingy.

- Difficulty making friends.

If you see three or four of these symptoms and feel they are out of the ordinary, discuss it with your ex. Talk to your child and if necessary involve your doctor. Devise a mechanism to work through this issue.

Relationship MOT

It may sound odd, but in my relationship with my new partner we carry out regular relationship MOTs. We talk about how things are going, things that make us happy and sad, and what we can do to make things even better between us, all of which keeps our relationship healthy. You should do the same with your children on a one-to-one basis.

The best way to do a dad and child MOT is to prepare:

● In your diary, regularly write things you'd like to discuss.

● Sit down with the TV off and explain that you want to talk about how things are going. Perhaps you can start by talking about the positive things that have been going on and then ask your child to tell you about some positive elements he or she has enjoyed.

● Then you can ask if you are doing anything the child does not like or would like changed.

● Then you can raise issues regarding the child's behaviour.

● At the end, make a list of things you each promise to do better and some more positive things you want to do together.

● At your next MOT, read through your last meeting notes and see if you have kept your promises.

I am told by many divorced dads that this system really works. Because it starts with positives and gives the child an equal forum with the parent, it helps improve your relationship and makes everyone feel confident about their status. The most important thing to remember is that these MOTs are not one-offs but should be done regularly and become part of your routine.

TOP TIPS FOR SUCCESSFUL LIVING AND LEARNING

- Be aware of your responsibilities. Do not expect your ex to do it; do it yourself, or agree a plan to reinforce what you have both taught your children.
- Living and learning issues discussed here are central to creating a well-rounded, happy and positive child. Divorced dads must make time to cover these areas and not shy away from the messy ones.
- Research your topics and have a list of organisations you can call for assistance. This includes the nursery, school, other carers and your GP.
- Do not be afraid to use a counsellor or parenting coach to help you and to provide extra independent support.
- Ask family and friends who have children how they handled things. Build up a support network and use it.
- Routine rules and consistency conquers, but be prepared to alter routines as children grow.
- Stick with it. You have to be prepared for problems, but be committed to overcoming them.
- Try to involve your ex-wife in all processes if at all possible. Put your children first and ensure you and your ex-wife present a united front.
- Use reward charts to monitor progress and provide your children with encouragement.
- Use the dad and child MOT as a way of building respect and communication with your children.
- Remember: you are not alone and there are many divorced dads going through the same thing.

Sources of Information

General advice on coping with divorce

www.advicenow.org.uk For advice on separation and divorce.

www.cafcass.gov.uk Child and Family Court Advisory and Support Service – looks after the interests of children involved in court proceedings.

www.citizensadvice.org.uk The Citizens Advice service helps people resolve their legal, money and other problems. If you are short of money, this is a good starting point to help plan how you are going to fund your divorce case and if you qualify for legal aid.

www.csa.gov.uk Child Support Agency used by parents to ensure their ex pays maintenance for care of the children.

www.direct.gov.uk This government website is a starting point for information about separation, divorce and your rights. Type Divorce in the search box.

www.dwp.gov.uk For advice on child support, pensions and benefits.

www.familymediationhelpline.co.uk Family mediation hotline.

www.lawsociety.org.uk/choosingandusing/findasolicitor.law Website set up by the Law Society that allows you to find relevant lawyers in the area.

www.legalservices.gov.uk Can assist with advice on legal aid and other issues relating to divorce.

www.ukcfm.co.uk UK College of Family Mediators, useful if you need mediation services.

Dads' support groups

http://dads-uk.co.uk/main/news.php Website set up to assist single and divorced dads.

www.equalparenting.org Organisation that supports equal parenting after divorce.

www.family2000.org.uk Website for all single, divorced and separated parents.

www.fathersdirect.com Information for dads on a range of subjects.

www.fnf.org.uk Family Needs Fathers – good for networking.

www.gingerbread.org.uk Organisation for one-parent families.

www.parentlineplus.org.uk Website designed to help anyone parenting children.

www.parentscentre.gov.uk Covers many questions from birth to teenage years.

www.relate.org.uk Excellent site for advice and support during separation and divorce.

General support groups

www.samaritans.org.uk 0845 790 9090 24-hour emotional support for anyone going through a personal crisis.

Useful books and magazines

Check with your local library or bookshop or buy online through **www.amazon.co.uk**

- *How to Help the Children Survive the Divorce* by Jody Beveridge and Alan Bradley, W. Foulsham & Co. Ltd
- *Control Your Divorce* by Jody Beveridge and Jan Bennett, W. Foulsham & Co. Ltd
- *How to Help Your Child Cope with Grief* by Janice Perkins, W. Foulsham & Co. Ltd
- *Was It the Chocolate Pudding?: A Story for Little Children About Divorce* by Sandra Levins and Bryan Langdo, Magination Press
- *Two Homes* by Claire Masurel, Walker Books Ltd

- *Dinosaurs Divorce: A Guide for Changing Families* (Paperback) by Laurene Krasny Brown and Marc Brown, Little, Brown Book Group
- *One Up* magazine for parents and step-parents: www.oneup magazine.co.uk

Making a home for your children

www.amazon.co.uk Online store for books and much more.

www.argos.co.uk Online version of the high street store.

www.asda.co.uk Online version of the high street store.

www.eBay.co.uk Online auction site.

www.maplin.co.uk For electronic equipment, including door alarms.

www.woolworths.co.uk Online version of the high street store.

Great places to get craft kits

http://parentingteens.about.com Great craft section as well as general advice.

www.craftmaterialsupplies.co.uk Great craft kits for children, including candle making and jewellery with instructions that are child and dad friendly.

www.elc.com Early Learning Centre. Online version of the high street store. Great for craft kits and bits and pieces.

www.elysian.co.uk/shop/fairies-fairy-gifts-children-c-45_89.html Great for fairy kits.

www.freekidcrafts.com/free_kid_craft_ideas.html Free children's crafts.

www.google.co.uk Google for 'toddler colouring pages' and you will find free printable colouring pages.

www.hobbycraft.co.uk Online version of the high street store, with a good children's section.

www.thecraftyhippo.co.uk A family-run business with good craft kits.

www.whsmith.co.uk Online version of the high street store.

www.woolworths.co.uk Online version of the high street store.

www.yellowmoon.org.uk Recommended by many schools and reasonably priced. You can order a catalogue and buy items separately or as kits.

Education

www.ofsted.gov.uk/reports Enter your postcode and then select nurseries, independent schools, state schools and special schools in the area and their reports and standings.

www.ucas.co.uk Central resources for information on undergraduate courses at colleges and universities.

Health and well-being

www.asthma.org.uk Offers help and advice for asthma sufferers and their carers.

www.childrenfirst.nhs.uk Interactive site on health for children and young people.

www.firstaidwarehouse.co.uk For first aid equipment and accessories, including first aid kits, health and safety posters, and home poison charts.

www.netdoctor.co.uk Patient-friendly site offering help and advice on a variety of health issues.

www.nhsdirect.nhs.uk 0845 4647 Free National Health Service advice.

www.nutrition.org.uk Website of the British Nutrition Foundation.

www.patient.co.uk Promises 'Comprehensive, free, up-to-date health information as provided by GPs to patients during consultations'.

www.sja.org.uk Website for St John Ambulance. Gives information about first aid courses for parents.

www.uclan.ac.uk/student_services/health/child-common.htm University of Central Lancashire resource on a variety of health issues, including childhood illnesses.

Holidays

www.airtours.co.uk Bargain family package holidays.

www.babyworld.co.uk/information/newparents/bargainholidays. asp For family holidays with babies.

www.butlins.com Family holidays for children of all ages.

www.dh.gov.uk/travellers To apply for a European Health Insurance Card (EHIC).

www.explore.co.uk/familyadventures Adventure and activity holidays for energetic families.

www.holidaylettings.co.uk/ideas.asp Website facilitating lettings of holiday villas and apartments direct from the owners.

www.lastminute.com Last-minute deals on holidays, hotels, travel and entertainment.

www.opodo.co.uk Online holiday booking agency.

www.responsibletravel.com Website for 'responsible and ecotourism holidays'.

www.summerfun4kids.co.uk Online directory of summer camps and holiday courses for unaccompanied children and teenagers.

Living and learning

Books on potty training
Once Upon a Potty: Girl/Once Upon a Potty: Boy by Alona Frankel, HarperFestival

Name tags
Some good websites to purchase tags online include:

www.minilabels.co.uk

www.nameitlabels.co.uk

www.wovenlabelsuk.com

Name tags are also available on eBay. Your school or nursery might also be able to suggest suppliers.

Laundry

www.ecover.com Ecological detergents and cleansing agents, available from health stores and some supermarkets.

Talking about sex

www.fpa.org.uk 020 7608 5240 Family Planning Association can provide leaflets and recommend books.

Let's Talk About Sex by Robbie Harris, Walker Books

Growing Up (Facts of Life) by Susan Meredith and Robyn Gee, Usborne Publishing Ltd

Asking about Sex and Growing Up: A Question-And-Answer Book for Boys and Girls by Joanna Cole, HarperTrophy

Drugs

http://hcd2.bupa.co.uk/fact_sheets/html/teen_drugs.html Advice on teenagers and drugs from health company BUPA.

www.ndh.org.uk 0800 776600 National Drugs Helpline for parents and children. Also accessible via **www.talktofrank.com**

Raising Drug-free children: 100 Tips for Parents by Aletha Solter, Da Capo Lifelong

Adolescent Drug and Alcohol Abuse: How to Spot It, Stop It and Get Help for Your Family by Nikki Babbit, O'Reilly

Index